THE FAITH OF JOHN KNOX

TO

MY WIFE

THE
FAITH
OF
JOHN KNOX

The Croall Lectures
for 1960

by

JAMES S. McEWEN

Professor of Church History
in the University of Aberdeen

JOHN KNOX PRESS
RICHMOND, VIRGINIA

Published in Great Britain by Lutterworth Press,
London, and in the United States of America by
John Knox Press, Richmond, Virginia.

Library of Congress Catalog Card Number 62-8020

PRINTED AND MADE IN GREAT BRITAIN BY
FLETCHER AND SON LTD NORWICH AND
THE LEIGHTON-STRAKER BOOKBINDING CO LTD LONDON

CONTENTS

Preface

THIS book contains the Croall Lectures which were delivered in New College, Edinburgh, early in 1960. The Croall Lecturer is required to deal with a theological subject; and the occasion—the opening of the quater-centenary year of the Scottish Reformation —dictated a subject connected with that event. It seemed to me that this was an opportunity to make some contribution to a curiously neglected task—the systematic study of John Knox's teaching.

It is strange that, even in Scotland, so little has been done in this field. Theologians appear to have assumed that Knox was a pious, and therefore undeviating, disciple of John Calvin with no distinctive opinions of his own, and that no separate study of his theology was required. I hope that the following pages, and particularly the chapter on the sacraments, will show that Knox was no mere echo of Calvin, but has something to say of his own that is worthy of attention.

Historians and literary writers seem to me to be prone to a rather different error in their references to Knox's religious views. They tend to read back into Knox the Calvinism of later times with which, perhaps, they are more familiar. They appear to ignore the fact that some of the main roots of later Scottish Calvinism run back not to Knox at all but to the English Puritanism of the Westminster Assembly era. It is important in this connexion to remember that the doctrinal standard of the Church of Scotland since 1647 has been the *Westminster Confession*, of which Principal Burleigh has rightly remarked that it presents "a Calvinism more rigid than Calvin's". It could be said with equal justice of the older *Scots Confession* of Knox's era, that it enshrines a Calvinism decidedly warmer and less rigid than Calvin's. It is therefore quite illegitimate to take later Scottish Calvinism— shaped as it was by the rigidities of the Westminster Confession—

as a fair representation of Knox's faith, or even as the logical development of Knox's faith. It is neither of these things: its parentage lies rather in the Westminster of 1647 than in the Edinburgh of 1560.

It may be remarked in passing that the same distinction exists between later Scottish worship and the worship of Knox's time. The *Westminster Directory* replaced *Knox's Liturgy*, and Scottish worship thereafter swung markedly away from the old tradition into close conformity with the English Puritan pattern.

Knox thus stands in a measure of isolation from Calvin on the one hand, and from later Scottish Calvinism on the other: and he must be allowed to speak for himself instead of being forced to speak in the tones of either Geneva or Westminster.

In these lectures I have tried to go to Knox's writings without dogmatic presuppositions, and to let him say for himself what he has to say. It has not been an easy task. Knox left very little systematic theological writing, and I have had to gather his teaching piecemeal from his pamphlets and letters, and to place my own stress on what seemed to me to be distinctive and important. And over a good deal of the worst ground I have had to break my own trail; for no one seemed to have travelled over quite the same ground before.

I have tried to keep in mind the general reader who may desire to gain some knowledge of Knox's teaching, but may not have special theological knowledge; and for that reason I have attempted in each chapter to place Knox's teaching against the general theological thought of his time, and to display the agreements and the differences. Some of those who patiently listened to the lectures were kind enough to say that they found them comprehensible even without specialized knowledge: I hope that those who may read them will find them not less so. I have retained the lecture-form with little alteration, believing that it adds a certain amount of liveliness to the treatment of the subject.

Many more footnotes could have been added; but there are, I think, sufficient to enable the general reader to check what I have written for himself if he desires to do so—and I hope he will. The expert can use them as signposts to the spots where I think I have picked up gold, and he can go there and do his own digging.

I offer this book in the conviction that there is more gold yet to be mined in John Knox. I have dug into theological ground just about as far as it is safe for a historian to go. I hope that some properly equipped theologian will now think it worth his while to take up the pick and shovel.

Aberdeen,
March 1961.

The Life of John Knox

OF Knox's early life we know almost nothing. He was born of humble parentage, probably about the year 1514, near the town of Haddington in East Lothian; and it is supposed that he received his training for the priesthood at the University of St Andrews. Apart from the two facts that he held the post of Apostolical Notary in the Haddington area and acted as tutor to the children of some gentlemen of East Lothian, his life is practically a blank until his brief association with the Reformer George Wishart in the winter of 1545–46. By Wishart he was apparently confirmed in Reforming opinions.

Almost a year after the assassination of Cardinal Beaton, Knox —on the instructions of his employers—took his pupils to St Andrews; and there the Protestants of the castle garrison compelled the reluctant schoolmaster to become a preacher of the Reformed faith. His pulpit utterances brought him immediate recognition as a leading spokesman of the Protestant cause; but the castle fell to a French fleet in 1547, and Knox spent the next nineteen months as a slave in the French galleys.

Early in 1549 he was released through the good offices of the English government; and that government employed him for the next five years as a preacher in various parts of England. As a vigorous preacher of Reform he became a recognized leader of the Puritan wing of English Protestantism, and a Royal chaplain. He was offered the bishopric of Rochester and the living of All-Hallows, London, but declined both appointments.[1]

On the accession of Mary Tudor, Knox escaped to the Continent where he became, first, minister of a congregation of English exiles at Frankfort, and subsequently minister of a strongly Puritan congregation of English refugees at Geneva. In the

[1] On Knox's work in England see Lorimer, *John Knox and the Church of England*, London, 1875.

autumn of 1555 he paid a visit to Scotland (his first since the fall of St Andrews Castle) during which he urged the Protestant nobility to prepare to take stronger and more united action in defence and furtherance of the Protestant cause.

Matters reached a crisis in Scotland in 1559. Elizabeth had seated herself insecurely on the English throne in 1558. France had her hands freed from other commitments by the Peace of Cateau Cambrésis early in 1559. The young Mary, Queen of Scots, became Queen also of France in July of the same year, and was—in Roman Catholic eyes—the rightful Queen of England as well. French ambition now regarded Scotland as the base for pressure on England with a view to driving the heretic Elizabeth from her throne and securing it for the young Catholic Queen of France and Scotland.

A prerequisite for the execution of this plan was the elimination of "disloyal" Scottish Protestantism; but the Regent of Scotland —Mary of Guise, mother of Mary Queen of Scots—underestimated Protestant strength and solidarity, and acted with insufficient French troops at her command. At the first signs of a move against them, the Protestants of Scotland mustered in arms and were joined by Knox. A year later, on the tardy arrival of English aid, the French were defeated and gave up the struggle, and the Protestants were left in control of Scotland. The Scottish Parliament abolished papal jurisdiction in 1560 and approved the *Scots Confession* as a statement of the faith now to be acknowledged in Scotland.

The next step should have been the organization and endowment of a Reformed Church. Knox, in high hopes, presented to Parliament his proposals in the form of the *First Book of Discipline*. The *Book* not only sketched a polity for the Reformed Church, but included schemes for poor-relief, the repair of derelict churches,[1] and the provision of universal compulsory education, free to the poor, from parish school right up to the university for all who showed ability to profit by it. These schemes, however,

---

[1] These were almost innumerable owing to English depredations and years of ecclesiastical negligence.

would have involved the use of the greater part of the endowments of the Old Church; and the majority in Parliament—already deeply involved in the traffic in Church lands and benefices—had no desire to see this source of wealth expended on Knox's "devout imaginings". Parliament accordingly rejected the *Book of Discipline*, and proceeded instead to life-rent in their benefices—though without spiritual functions—all Roman Catholic clergy who were prepared to live peaceably under the new Protestant regime, with the proviso that they should pay over a proportion of their revenues to the crown. The crown, after meeting its own expenses, would dole out the residue to the Reformed Church.

Knox and his fellow-Reformers were thus confronted with the fact that they could expect little support, either legal or financial, from the government in their efforts to organize a Reformed Church. This certainly set them free to follow out more extreme patterns of Reform than any government would have been likely to sanction; but it also drove the Reformed Church, and Knox its leader, into a position of chronic opposition to the government, and laid the train for all the explosions of religious strife in the next century and a half.

The return of the youthful Queen Mary to occupy the throne of her ancestors in 1561 did nothing to mend matters. The country needed a strong Protestant ruler: it got a young Catholic Queen who neither could nor would take strong action to settle a Protestant religious establishment—who was indeed privately pledged to seek its ultimate overthrow. The situation was an impossible one for all the leading actors in it: for Mary, for the temporizing Protestant politicians, and for Knox. Knox may of course be blamed for his recourse to demagogy which heaped fuel on the smouldering fires of dissension; but it is hard to see what other line of action he could have been expected to take at this time. He feared Mary—feared her all the more for that charm which made her the magnetic centre of a growing Catholic revival: and he utterly distrusted (not without good reason) the Protestant politicians who were her early advisers. To whom, then, could he look for the defence of the Reformed Church? Its only strength now lay with the commons; and Knox now used all the influence of the pulpit to keep the commons roused and alert for its defence. This, of course, roused the wrath of the politicians, and Knox's former allies among the nobility pled with him for moderation; but Knox could see no safety for Protestantism in their brand of "moderation", and parted company with them in bitterness. Mary, naturally, was infuriated by Knox's meddling with politics and attempted in vain to have him condemned for treason.

The last ten years of Knox's life were thus unhappy, anxious, and bitter with disillusionment. The Reformed Church which he had hoped to see strong and prosperous, working amicably with a Reformed Parliament under the favouring eye of a Protestant ruler for the blessing of the people, was instead struggling into half-existence, hampered by poverty, and thwarted at every turn by government apathy or even open hostility. Towards the close of Mary's reign, and in the turbulent years that followed, its continued existence seemed at times problematical; and Knox—a dying man—had again to flee from Edinburgh. The hospitals for the sick poor on which he had set his heart, which were to have been provided from monastic revenues, were forever impossible— the revenues all gone. The schools that were to have dotted the land, and the streams of eager young scholars who were to have gone up to the universities to make Scotland a land of learning and of light—these too were visions faded beyond all hope of recall. The reality on which Knox closed his eyes in death in 1572 was a Kirk still ill-organized, impoverished, tempest-tossed, with its future black with uncertainty—and a land bleeding from the wounds of civil war.

Unhappy is the reformer who lives beyond the hour of triumph, to see the inevitable tarnishing of his visions, and to grow bitter in disillusionment. Knox should have died in 1560 when the bells of Edinburgh were ringing out for the great Protestant victory; but history is an untidy business, and anticlimax is of the very stuff of human life. The bitterness of those

latter years tarnished not only Knox's visions, but also his reputation; and there are those who judge that the Reformed Church in
those years would have fared better without his vehemence, and
under the guidance of more politic men. That judgment may be
questioned. In turbulent times politic men make poor leaders; and
politic men, and their causes, fared but ill in other departments of
Scottish life in those evil days. If the trumpet had not sounded,
and kept on sounding, would the Kirk Reformed have stayed the
brunt of battle? It may well be doubted.

Yet here lies the tragedy of Knox's life—that he coveted peace,
but lived and died in strife: that his last years were saddened by
tarnished visions and shattered hopes: that he saw with dreaming
gaze a Promised Land, but found not the means to lead his people
into it.

Biographies of Knox

THE biographies by Thomas McCrie and Hume Brown are still standard works. The best edition of McCrie is that published in Edinburgh in 1855. Hume Brown's biography in two volumes was published in London in 1895 and contains a wealth of historical annotation. Recent research, however, has called in question most of what they have written of Knox's early life prior to 1545.

For a more modern factual account in shorter compass, the reader may consult Henry Cowan's volume in the *Heroes of the Reformation* series (New York and London, 1905).

Andrew Lang's *John Knox and the Reformation*, also published in 1905, has the avowed aim of pulling down the Calvinist saint from his pedestal. On the historical side the book contains much of solid value; but Lang had a scanty acquaintance with Calvinist theology, and no sympathy whatever with what he thought he knew of it, and to that extent he fails to give an illuminating interpretation of Knox.

Edwin Muir's *John Knox* (London, 1929) is not so much a biography as a sustained sneer. It has a considerable vogue among those who confuse historical criticism with mere malice; but the discriminating reader may feel that the author has failed to discern the stature of his victim.

Incomparably the best modern biography of Knox is that by Lord Eustace Percy (London, 1937). Percy displays keen and sensitive historical and theological insight, and the portrait of Knox which emerges—in his greatness and littleness, his weakness and strength—is valid and convincing. I have been much indebted to Percy in the preparation of these lectures.

Two recently published sketches of Knox—*Plain Mr. Knox* by Elizabeth Whitley and *The Thundering Scot* by Geddes McGregor—may be more readily accessible than some of the works listed above, though they cannot be regarded as adequate alternatives to Percy or the older biographies.

On Calvinism

FOR the general reader there is no better book than J. T. McNeill's *History and Character of Calvinism* (New York, 1954 and Oxford University Press), which presents a lucid survey of the history of Calvinism and of its doctrines from the Reformation to the present day. I desire to acknowledge my indebtedness to Dr McNeill, particularly for insights and for quotations used in the chapter on Providence.

Knox's Works

KNOX'S collected Works are available in the edition by David Laing—*The Works of John Knox* (Edinburgh; Wodrow Society, 1846–64, 6 Vols.).

Knox's *History of the Reformation in Scotland* is, of course, included in Laing's edition of the collected *Works*; but it has recently (1949) become available in a magnificent edition of two volumes by Professor W. Croft Dickinson.

All footnotes referring to Knox's *Works* in this book are to Laing's edition. Footnotes referring to his *History* are to Dickinson's edition.

The *Scots Confession* and the *Book of Discipline* are included in both Laing's *Works* and Dickinson's *History*.

1

THE FAITH BEFORE KNOX

1

The Faith before Knox

EVENTS such as the Reformation in Scotland, which was carried through in the fourteen months between May, 1559, and July, 1560, may happen with the suddenness of a lightning flash, but they do not happen without antecedents. And commonly, the more sudden and dramatic the event, the further back do its roots go into history: there has been a slow building up of pressures, which only await some signal for the catastrophic release of their potential.

The arrival of Knox in Scotland in May, 1559, was the signal for the release of these pent up forces; but the forces, complex in origin and type, had been gradually building up for almost two hundred years. Political, social, moral and religious factors were all involved.

Political motives undoubtedly played a large part in preparing the way for, and carrying through, the Reformation: but since our concern in these lectures is with matters of faith, the barest outline of these political factors will have to suffice.

The Stuart Kings, from James I to James V, had been involved in a constant struggle for power with the great nobles. This conflict between nobility and crown began to have religious implications in the reign of James V; for James, having alienated a good many of his temporal lords by his efforts to assert royal authority in his turbulent kingdom, was compelled to rely more and more on the support of the lords spiritual—and to do this just at the time when Henry of England had broken with the Pope, and was reducing the great Churchmen to complete subservience.

The consequences of this alliance of crown and church against the nobility were, first of all, bad blood and jealousy between a considerable faction of the nobility and the Churchmen who were gathering power and influence into their hands. A second consequence was that the disaffected nobles did what disaffected nobles in Scotland had done for centuries: turned to England for comfort and support. They turned to England all the more hopefully because King Henry was now at daggers drawn with the Pope's Church; and for that same reason they were not disappointed in their expectations of English support.

The Churchmen, on the other hand, saw in France—the old ally of Scotland, the Catholic power, the traditional enemy of England—their hope of salvation. Beaton, the leader of the Scottish Church, had been a diplomat in France, was in high favour with the French King, and had been rewarded with the tenure of certain French benefices, the emoluments of which formed a substantial part of his income. Thus he was as much in French pay as the "Assured Lords"[1] were in English pay, and perhaps even more unscrupulously determined to utilize Scotland as a pawn in the French game, than the "Assured Lords" were to sell out to England.

To the generality of Scotsmen, loyalty to the crown, hostility to England, and traditional friendship with France, made the Church's policy seem the patriotic one. In such circumstances, a general movement towards Protestantism—the "English religion" —was not to be expected: and the Church was able, from time to time, to exact from the crown stern measures for the suppression of heresy.

The disasters resulting from Beaton's reckless anti-English policy, followed by the gradual realization that French suzerainty was bidding fair to become a worse menace to Scottish independence than any threat that was likely to come from England, caused an increasing revulsion of feeling against the Church and the French alliance. But revulsion against the Church and France inevitably meant increasing favour for Protestantism and England. In 1560, an English expeditionary force ejected the French expeditionary force from Scottish soil—probably just in the nick of time

[1] The name given to Scottish nobles who were in receipt of English subsidies.

for the preservation of Scottish independence: and the future of Scotland lay with Protestantism, and an eventual union of the Scottish and English crowns.

Among social factors leading towards the Reformation there must be mentioned the rising importance—and conscious importance—of the lesser lairds, and of the burgher class, which resulted mainly from expanding trade. Lifted above the grinding poverty of the poor labourers, and therefore with leisure to think; with at least a smattering of education—and in the case of some of the lairds a very good education; schooled by trading to make shrewd judgments of men and events, and to act on their judgments; accustomed as burghers and magistrates to take responsibility and to exercise authority—this was the class which was becoming the solid backbone of the nation, and this was the class from which came the most solid support of the Reformation; not only in Scotland, but wherever in Europe Reform occurred. In England, this rising class became politically vocal in the House of Commons. The Scottish Parliament made no provision for their representation, being wholly feudal in composition: had it done so, King and Commons together might have enforced some needed reformation in the Church a good deal sooner than it came.

For this class was, on the whole, sharply critical of the Church. The gross maladministration of the Church, and the rampant ecclesiastical peculations, offended all its instincts of commercial integrity and good management. The notorious immorality, all too common in all ranks of the clergy and the monastic orders, offended that ingrained moralism which (so we are told) is the mark of the bourgeois wherever you find him. And priestly ignorance, which was also undoubtedly widespread, excited their contempt.

When a rival faith was presented to their minds, they weighed the Old Church in the balance, found it sadly wanting, and with remarkable unanimity turned their backs upon it. The Reformed Church gave them much that they valued—not least a substantial part in the management of its affairs. And its General Assembly became, in some measure, that House of Commons which the Scottish Parliament did not possess. Thus, through the Reformation, this social class found a means of fulfilling some, at least, of its ambitions.

At the upper end of the social scale the nobility, as we have seen, were anxious to oust the Churchmen from high posts of government. Further, the Scottish nobility were not, on the whole, wealthy—and the Church was. There was material enough here to induce many a nobleman to take serious thought about ecclesiastical matters.

At the opposite end of the scale, times were cruelly hard for the poor, and various ecclesiastical exactions pressed harshly upon them. In countries where the Church was better administered the monasteries were often the friends of the poor, and the monks well beloved. In Scotland, however, there was widespread maladministration, and not many monasteries were capable of being, either financially or spiritually, homes of charity to the poor. Lands and revenues which had been left to the monastic orders by pious donors for the behoof of the poor were often mercilessly devoured by absentee abbots, and even by laymen who held office *in commendam* in defiance of acts of the Scottish Parliament against the practice; and every last penny had to be exacted from the poor tenants of monastic lands to satisfy the voracity of these parasites. Little attention was paid by such overlords to the discipline and well-being of the religious communities whose revenues they lived upon: and Lesley, earnest Romanist though he was, has left a dark description of Scottish monastic life as he personally knew it. When the Reformation brought the downfall of the monasteries, the lot of the poor was certainly not worsened thereby; and Scotland staged no Pilgrimage of Grace in their defence.

These, then, are some of the main political and social pressures which were building up towards the final explosion of 1559–60. On the whole, they are well documented and well known. But when we turn to an examination of the religious factors making towards Reform, we are in difficulties at once: for men who entertained heretical opinions before the Reformation took care not to advertise the fact—for obvious reasons. And what was carefully concealed from the prying eyes of ecclesiastical inquisitors at the time cannot be uncovered by the historians of later centuries. The most part of the evidence is gone beyond recovery. Occasionally, however, some unfortunate heretic was caught and the evidence against him recorded; or enactments were made against heresies, from which we can presume that they were in existence. These events are, as it were, the mountain peaks rising above the mists, from which we can make some guesses at the lie of the land between. As we come towards the Reformation itself our information becomes fuller, and we can make a better picture. Information about orthodox religious observance is naturally more plentiful, and from it we can deduce some understanding of the normal piety of the times.

It is significant that the first reports of heresy in Scotland appear towards the end of the great Papal Schism. In the early mediaeval period, a powerful Papacy had rendered valuable service in checking the secularization of the Church all over Europe, and in securing the appointment to high ecclesiastical position of able men, truly devoted to the welfare of the Church. From the death of Innocent III in 1216, however, Papal power declined steadily to its practical eclipse in the Babylonish Captivity which began in 1309. Then in 1378 the Papal Schism began, and lasted until 1415 —or, so far as Scotland was concerned, 1418; for Scotland was slow to withdraw allegiance from the last surviving anti-Pope.

These years of the Papal Schism were ruinous for the Church in Scotland, but were haymaking weather for the Scottish crown and nobility; for the Church was the one road to wealth in Scotland at that time. We know that in 1550, or thereby, half the revenue of Scotland was in the hands of the Church: and Dr Gordon Donaldson has estimated ecclesiastical revenues about that time as approximately three hundred thousand pounds a year, while crown revenues were only a beggarly seventeen thousand pounds odd.[1] The proportion cannot have been much different a century or so earlier.

Rival Popes therefore, outbidding one another for Scottish support, vied in granting dispensations for all sorts of irregular appointments to ecclesiastical livings, and for other breaches of Canon Law—not to mention the rules of common decency. Wealthy benefices became the prey of the crown and the nobility, as rewards to favourites, and as the only possible way in which younger sons and royal bastards could be provided with an adequate living. Men with no spiritual interests, and often with no administrative aptitudes, were thus thrust into high ecclesiastical offices: and (not surprisingly) the discipline of the Church was disastrously slackened, and both the secular clergy and the monastic orders sank into laxity and sloth. The lower ecclesiastics also fell into abject poverty; for so much money was milked off at the upper levels that there was little left for the work of the parishes or the day-to-day life of the monasteries.

The end of the Papal Schism brought no improvement; for an impoverished Papacy, desperate for funds to rehabilitate itself, was prepared to connive at such irregular appointments in consideration of receiving a "cut" out of the takings. Thus, despite local and temporary improvements here and there under the few good Churchmen who appeared, the general laxity and sloth continued right down to the Reformation.

It was the besetting vice of the royal House of Stuart—of the Five Jameses—that although they were well aware of the scandalous state of the Church, and from time to time with a great show of indignation demanded of the Churchmen that they should put their house in order, yet they themselves continued unabated, and were the chief patterns and exemplars to others, in the practice of intruding unspiritual men into the highest ecclesiastical offices.[2] There could be no reform in the Church until this practice was stopped; and neither Crown nor Papacy evinced any desire to put an end to it.

[1] *Thirds of Benefices* (Scottish History Society).
[2] R. K. Hannay, *The Scottish Crown and the Papacy*, (Historical Association of Scotland, Pamphlet N.S. 6.)

It was during the latter part of the Papal Schism that Wyclif was at work in England: and within twenty years of his death there were Lollards in Scotland. In 1406 the Lollard priest Resby was caught and burned in Perth. That he was not an isolated bird of passage is shown by Bower's remark that he was "held in much esteem for his preaching to simple folk." Bower also tells us that forty years later, when he was writing, Lollard views were still secretly held and propagated: and he speaks quaintly of these heretics "flying like dragons through their native land on the surface of the Scriptures."[1]

The reference to Resby's preaching to the simple folk may be significant: for Wyclif's attack on the wealth and greedy exactions of Churchmen was bound to be acceptable to many commoners. But Lollardy had been ruined in England by its supposed connexion with the social unrest which led to the Peasant Revolt of 1381; and for that reason it was no doubt viewed with suspicion by the government as well as the Church in Scotland. Certainly in 1425 it was Parliament which passed an act requiring all bishops to make diligent search for heretics—which must mean Lollards.

In 1433, or thereabouts, the Hussite emissary Paul Craw[2] was apprehended at St Andrews University. The Hussites at this time were attempting to cement relationships with sympathizers all over Europe, and Craw's visit to Scotland is not to be interpreted as a missionary venture so much as an embassy to sympathizers who were known to exist. When we take this along with the oath against Lollardy imposed on Arts students in St Andrews as early as 1416, and with Bishop Kennedy's endowment of St Salvator's College in St Andrews as a training place for learned clergy urgently required to combat pestilential heresy, we may reasonably deduce that Lollardy was endemic in that part of Eastern Scotland from the first decade of the fifteenth century: and that it continued to exist—with how much strength we have no means of knowing—until it was superseded by Lutheranism a hundred years later.

The celebrated case of the Lollards of Kyle in 1494 gives

---

[1] *Scotichronicon*, XV, 20.   [2] Or Crawar—a Scottish attempt at a Czech name.

evidence of considerable Lollard penetration in the south-west of Scotland. Hay Fleming[1] quotes cases, and traditions such as that of Murdoch Nisbet, which tend to show that family Bible reading in the vernacular, and anti-clerical beliefs similar to Lollardy, were of long standing in this part of Ayrshire. And Knox describes it as "a receptacle of God's servants of old".

Actually, the Church's fear of Lollardy was probably exaggerated, for it was overwhelmingly a negative movement—and Reformations are not made out of negatives. Its articles of faith were a list of thunderous denials of accepted doctrine and practice; but positive affirmation was scanty. Even its cultivation of Bible reading was desultory and ineffective, for Lollardy scarcely penetrated to a unifying grasp of Scripture: no one doctrine, such as Justification by Faith, served as a focal point to draw all Scripture together into a meaningful and dynamic whole. Bower spoke more truly than he knew when he described the Lollards as flying like dragons on the *surface* of Scripture.

The contribution of Lollardy to the Scottish Reformation lay, probably, not in anything positive; but in fostering and spreading a critical attitude to Church doctrine and practice—apparently among all classes of society. But we do not really know how widespread or how strong the movement was; and its contribution, even on this negative aspect, is hard to assess. Possibly it was not great.

There was one point at which the Church rightly discerned a special menace in Lollard teaching: the Lollard doctrine that he alone is a true priest who is morally and spiritually worthy of his office. If that were accepted, the Church's whole scheme of salvation would fall to bits, and no man could be certain of his salvation. For salvation was believed to depend on the grace received through the sacraments: and the grace of the sacraments depended on their celebration by a true priest. If true priesthood was constituted, not by due ordination, but by moral and spiritual fitness, then only God who sees the secrets of men's hearts could tell whether any sacrament was valid. No man could ever be sure

[1] *The Reformation in Scotland*, p. 27ff.

that he was receiving a valid sacrament to his soul's salvation.

Probably a realization of this militated against the popularity of Lollard teaching among pious laymen, for who wants to exchange certainty for scepticism on such a vital matter? Reform awaited a new doctrine of grace, and of the sacraments, before it could move forward. The voice of Luther was required.

Meantime, popular piety still found it tolerable to make its home within the framework of the Church, thanks to the revival which took place among the Mendicant Orders—the Dominicans and the Observant section of the Franciscans. This revival began on the Continent fairly early in the 15th century, and was well established by the middle decades. It was characterized by austerity and purity of life, some resuscitation of learning, pastoral concern, and a great stress on preaching—the matter of the preaching being partly moralistic and partly a popularization of Church doctrine and of the cult of the Virgin. The message of the Mendicants was in no sense evangelical, as we to-day understand it. They preached hell and purgatory with terrifying power—and the sacraments of the Church, and pilgrimages and self-afflictions, as the only possible means of escape from the wrath to come. But they were in earnest, and they were clean. Men infinitely preferred them to the secular clergy for whom they had scant respect. The most coveted indulgences at this time were those that permitted the holder to by-pass his parish priest, and to make confession to, and receive his communion from, one of the preaching friars.[1]

In Scotland, this revival lasted not much more than a generation, but it did much good while it lasted—though constantly hampered by the jealousy of the regular ecclesiastics. The first Observants were brought into Scotland by James I from Holland in 1447, after his plea for reform in the monasteries had utterly failed to produce fruit. A handful of Observants, perhaps never more than five dozen of them, did good work out of all proportion to their numbers. The better bishops, such as Brown in

[1] See, for example, the Bull *Liquet Omnibus*, §3 and §8.

Dunkeld and Kennedy in St Andrews, used them to provide some sort of religious care for desolate and neglected parishes—of which there were literally hundreds. The burghers built friaries for the Observants and gathered in numbers to hear them—listening with heartfelt approval while the Observants, with the holy glee of conscious superiority, lashed the vices of the regular clergy: or listening with trembling dread as these skilled preachers uncovered the sinfulness of men's hearts and the inevitable consequence thereof, unless averted by all the means of grace that Holy Church could supply.

James IV styled himself "Protector of the Observants", and was wholly devoted to them, believing the salvation of Scotland, no less than of his own soul, to lie in their hands.

He was himself typical of the piety fostered by this movement,[1] both in its strength and its incredible weakness. He transacted no public business without first hearing two masses. He observed Sunday rigidly, and did much to make Scotland singular in Europe for Sabbatarianism. All fasts and feasts he strictly observed. His charitable offerings were costly. Every Easter season he retired to the Observant friary at Stirling, and spent Holy Week in absolute seclusion, in fasting and self-torture. He was a frequent pilgrim to Whithorn of St Ninian, and to St Duthac's shrine at Tain. Yet wherever he went—even on these pious pilgrimages—he took with him his substantial harem of mistresses, prayed and tortured himself at the shrine all day, and returned to them at night. His immorality was a public scandal; and his trafficking in Church benefices and his promotion of disgraceful favourites to ecclesiastical positions were an outrage upon the Church.

He was a man with a diseased and cankered conscience, and the only Gospel the best men in the Church had was one that harped incessantly on that damaged string. They had no word of sure comfort for this distraught soul, no liberating assurance of the forgiving love of God, no word of power to set him free, and few examples of clean-living clerics by which to encourage him. Those who talk about the coming of "gloomy Calvinism" to

---

[1] See A. R. MacEwen, *A History of the Church in Scotland*, Vol. I, p. 390f.

Scotland know nothing of the black terrors of the soul which it dispelled.

It was just as the Observant Movement declined, that Lutheranism began to enter Scotland: indeed, some of the best of the friars went over to it. By showing men that the grace of God was not tied to sacraments celebrated by a Roman priest, it made possible a piety that began to move a little aside from the official Church. Its message of the redeeming love of God, freely offered to men, had infinite appeal to souls darkened by the dread of God's wrath. Its central doctrine of Justification gave men a light by which to read and understand the Bible. A piety independent of the official Church was now possible, and began—very slowly—to take shape.

Within eight years of the beginning of Luther's Reforming activity, his works were circulating so freely in eastern Scotland that Parliament felt it necessary in 1525 to prohibit their importation, and to ban all discussion of his views. The gentle Patrick Hamilton perhaps did more by his death[1] than by his life to call attention to the new faith, and to engage men's sympathies, not only for him, but for the message he had died for. "Wherefore was he burned?" men asked: and Tyndale's New Testament, which began to reach Scotland in quantity just about the time of Hamilton's martyrdom, gave them the opportunity to compare the claims of the persecuting Church with the teaching of the Word of God.

The penetration of Lutheranism into Eastern Scotland was substantial; and many of those who afterwards became leaders in the Reformation received their early nurture from the Lutheran faith—men like Erskine of Dun, Balnaves, and probably Knox himself. To this we may trace the experientialism and evangelical warmth which were the distinguishing characteristics of the Scottish form of Calvinism: for those who know both the Calvinism of the *Institutes* and the Calvinism of the *Scots Confession*— the Church of Geneva and the Church of Scotland—are well

[1] Martyred at St. Andrews in 1528.

aware of deep differences, as well as of deep identities, between them.

Yet Lutheranism was curiously ineffective as a Reforming force. One reason may be that it was batting on a bad wicket. Throughout James V's reign anti-English feeling was strong; and Protestantism was the "English Religion". Another reason is that Lutheranism, while it inculcates personal piety, is politically quietist. Politics are for princes and governments. It is a fact that Lutheranism never made headway except under the fostering hand of a favourable prince. There was no favourable prince in Scotland to foster it: its only hope would have been the conversion of Mary of Guise,[1] and that did not occur. Calvinism did not supplant Lutheranism in Scotland: it simply succeeded where Lutheranism had failed.

One other attempt was made to present an alternative to Calvinism before the final cataclysm. In a last desperate effort to stave off the Reformation, Archbishop Hamilton, Beaton's unhappy successor, issued a series of statutes aimed at much-needed reform in the Church, and the suppression of clerical immorality. At the same time he put out a Catechism—perhaps composed by Wynram who later co-operated with Knox in writing the *Scots Confession*. The Catechism was for the instruction of ignorant priests in the faith. It does not mention the Pope: and while mainly Roman, it contains certain evangelical insights. Had all this been done, and done half a century earlier, Scotland might have had a Reformation after the Anglican type. But it came far too late: and even when it came, it effected nothing. The clergy laughed at such moral instructions from an archbishop who himself continued a notoriously profligate life, and matters went on as before—if not worse. The Church would not reform, and everyone knew it would not reform. It was incapable of producing any tolerable alternative to the Reformation: and it remained in its degradation to the last minute of its existence.

By 1546, however, the Swiss type of Reforming thought had

[1] Mother of Mary, Queen of Scots, and Regent of Scotland from 1554 to 1560.

begun to penetrate Scotland through George Wishart. It was much more uncompromising than Lutheranism, following Zwingli's tendency to reject all rites and ceremonies not explicitly sanctioned by Scripture. Under its influence, therefore, those who held Reforming sentiments were more inclined to separate themselves from the official Church; and the face of a Reformed Church began, though still in shadowy fashion, to emerge.

It was not before time; for the scandals of the Old Church had brought religion itself into disrepute. There is evidence of widespread neglect of all religion, and of the development of a scoffing contempt of it among a large section of the population.[1] Few troubled even to go to Mass. There was not only a Reformation to be carried through, but a reconversion of a land half-paganized, and debased in morality by the long evil example of its clergy.

Calvinism came in, in full tide, with Knox. With its conviction that one's duty is not to wait for history to be made, but rather to go and make history, it was the faith that was demanded by the hour.

And 1559 was the eleventh hour for the Reformation in Scotland, politically as well as spiritually. The Old Church was on the point of receiving such military aid from France as would suffice to establish it unshakably—and would suffice, too, for the complete extirpation of the Protestant faith, beyond hope of recovery.

There was no other faith in the field; no conceivable alternative. Scotland must go on to Calvinism, or back permanently to Rome. In 1559 it was Knox, or nothing.

For a fuller treatment of the historical matter summarized in this chapter, see Burleigh, *A Church History of Scotland*, London, 1960; or, in greater detail, MacEwen, *A History of the Church in Scotland*, 2 Vols., London, 1913.

[1] There is ample evidence of all this in the complaints of contemporary Churchmen— e.g. Statute 245 of 1551-2, in *Statutes of the Scottish Church*, Scottish History Society, Edinburgh 1907.

2

THE BIBLE
AND THE HOLY SPIRIT

2

The Bible and the Holy Spirit

IT is generally and rightly understood that the rediscovery of the Bible was one of the well-springs of the Reformation, and that the chief weapon of the Reformers in their contest with Rome and the Papacy was their assertion of the paramount authority of Holy Scripture. But perhaps the nature of that rediscovery of the Bible is not so well understood as it should be. Certainly the nature of the authority which the Reformers found in the Bible is very generally misunderstood.

The rediscovery of the Bible at the Reformation denotes a great deal more than the fact that it began to be read by masses of people who had never previously looked into it. Much more than that, it means that they read the Bible with new eyes and a new spirit. We do not comprehend the part played by the Bible in the Reformation until we realize how great is the abyss that yawns between the mediaeval view of the Bible and the Reformed view. It must be frankly admitted that the Reformers sometimes achieve the apparently impossible gymnastic exercise of straddling the abyss, with one foot on one side, and one on the other. Yet the abyss is there; and though the Reformers often teeter perilously on the brink of it, they do belong—quite decisively—to the other side of it from the mediaevalists. If we perceive the existence of this abyss, we shall be saved from such a superficial judgment as Andrew Lang's: that, in his attitude to, and use of, Scripture, John Knox was as complete a mediaevalist as his master John Major! As we shall see, Knox could put one foot back to the mediaeval side of the abyss when it suited him to do so. Luther and Calvin could do the same. But Knox, like Luther and Calvin, belonged to the other side of the gulf.

We shall also have to take account of the widespread and persistent misunderstanding of the nature of the authority which the Reformers—Knox among them—found in the Bible. It is too frequently assumed that the Reformers (since they lived in days before Higher Criticism sowed tares of doubt in the fields of Holy Scripture) must have been simple Biblical literalists who rather naively substituted an infallible Book for an infallible Pope: and thus that Mary Queen of Scots astutely pointed out the Achilles heel of Protestantism during her first interview with Knox, when she remarked that Scripture alone cannot be the final authority in religion, since the most divergent interpretations can be placed on vital texts by men of differing opinions.[1] To erect Scripture as the final authority is therefore to open the way to complete anarchy in religious matters.

Roman Catholic controversialists, from Mary's day to our own, have scarcely felt it necessary to move from Mary's position —pointing out, with grim satisfaction, the fulfilment of her prophecy in the tragic multiplication of Protestant divisions, all claiming Biblical authority for their particular variation of doctrine or practice. "From the unwholesomeness of the fruit," says Archbishop Spalding,[2] "we Catholics are abundantly satisfied of the unsoundness of the root." Within Protestantism itself, too, there are those who feel that the advance of critical studies has shaken, beyond repair, that confidence in the infallibility of Scripture on which they imagine the Reformation to have been founded. How anyone can imagine that the Reformation was founded on a simple Biblical literalism, or in blank ignorance of Higher Critical questions, is a mystery, when Luther's *Preface to the New Testament* provides open and abundant proof to the contrary.

Perhaps a reconsideration of some of Knox's writings, and of his practices, will help to clarify the Reformed understanding of the Bible and of its authority, and may even give us a small

---

[1] Knox, *History of the Reformation in Scotland* (edit. Dickinson), vol. II, p. 14ff.
[2] *History of Protestant Reformation*, Vol. I, p. 311ff.

glimmer of light on the way out of the scandal of our Protestant divisions.

But before we embark on this, we have to clear some ground at our starting-point. It is necessary to know how the Bible was regarded in the mediaeval Church before we can understand the Protestant reaction to this mediaeval view. And to understand the mediaeval view, we must take a brief backward glance to earlier times.

Down to the end of the 4th century A.D., the reading of the Bible was a duty enjoined upon all Christians; at least on all who could read, which possibly meant the majority of them. To study the "Memoirs and Letters of the Apostles"—the Gospels and Epistles—was considered to be a very necessary part of Christian edification.[1]

Athanasius, about the middle of the 4th century, complains that there are heretics who prevent their converts from reading the Bible: not so the Catholic Church. And a little later Chrysostom urges laymen to be more diligent in the study of Scripture, and not to leave it to monks and clerics. Thus, down to the end of the 4th century we find the laity being strongly encouraged to study the Bible.

It was no change of mind on the part of Church leaders that put an end to Bible study by the laity. It was the barbarian invasions of the 5th century, and the Dark Ages which followed after them, that brought about the eclipse of the Bible—for the simple and sufficient reason that the laity of the Church ceased to be able to read. For centuries the Western Church became a mission to an illiterate population, the laity being wholly dependent on the clergy for their acquaintance, at second-hand, with the Bible.

When at last learning revived, and a literate laity began gradually to appear again, the Church's attitude to Scripture had changed—and changed so greatly that, instead of welcoming the chance to restore the Bible to the laity, the Church regarded it with genuine misgiving. What had been considered a whole-

[1] Origen considers that Christians should spend one or two hours daily in private prayer and Bible study (Hom. II, *In Num.*, Vol. X, p. 19). See also Jerome, *Adv. Rufin.* I, ix.

some and indeed necessary study for laymen in the first four centuries of the Church's life was now regarded as a pursuit fraught with grave spiritual peril. We shall see the reason for this in a moment.

Despite the Church's new suspicion of the Bible, there was no general prohibition of Bible study during the Middle Ages. But there were local prohibitions. The Church duly noted that heretical sects like the Cathari, the Waldenses, the Wyclifites and the Hussites, were nurtured on the study of Scripture by laymen. In areas infected by such heresies, Bible reading was therefore stringently prohibited from the 13th century onwards. Elsewhere archbishops issued local prohibitions from time to time, if heresy was suspected to be on the increase. And everywhere Bible reading was regarded with considerable suspicion, as a risky pursuit, only too likely to seduce its devotees from the path of orthodoxy. The trial of the parish priest of Dollar, Thomas Forret, shows how proof of Bible reading, even by a priest, was regarded as an aggravating and damning piece of evidence against one accused of heresy.[1]

How is this new suspicion of the Bible to be accounted for? Dobschütz is superficial when he says it was simply part of the system for keeping the laity dependent on the priesthood.[2] No doubt that motive operated; but it was not the main motive.

Nor was discouragement of Bible reading simply a practical expedient for the keeping down of heresy. That motive did operate when heresy was rife, as in Scotland before 1560. But the true reason lay deeper. It was this: that the Bible had become, to the mediaeval Church, a bewildering and dangerous book. He who read it put his immortal soul in peril. Pope Innocent III, writing about the year 1210 to the Bishop of Metz, put the Church's attitude very clearly:—

"No doubt it is a laudable thing that a man should aspire to study for himself the oracles of God in Scripture. But the task is so difficult, the possibilities of error so great, and the consequences

[1] Calderwood, *History of the Kirk of Scotland*, Vol. I, p. 127ff; and Pitscottie (S.T.S. i.350).
[2] *Encyclopaedia of Religion and Ethics*, Vol. 2, p. 608.

of error so terrible, that no man should embark on such study unless he has prepared himself for it by a thorough training in theology."[1]

Here is the real reason for the mediaeval Church's fear of Bible reading—"the task of understanding it is so difficult; the possibility of error so great; the consequences of error so terrible." The Bible is now regarded as a baffling and dangerous book.

Contrast with this Knox's letter to Scotland in 1556,[2] insisting that lairds, burgesses and even artisans may sit down with the Bible; and together, even without the guidance of a minister, learn the truth of God from its pages. There is indeed a great gulf here between the mediaeval and the Reformed attitude to Scripture; so great indeed, that we may say that mediaevalist and Reformer, when they use the word "Scripture", mean by it two quite different things.

Now let us examine the difficulty, and the danger, which the mediaevalist saw in the Bible.

The difficulty was largely the result of the earlier threefold, and later fourfold, sense that was supposed to be discoverable in Scripture. Every text, in addition to its plain meaning which was the least important, had at least two, or possibly three, other hidden meanings which were very important indeed; but which could be unearthed only by the skilful use of allegory and typology.

Origen had found his threefold interpretation of Scripture very useful in constructing his synthesis of Platonism and Christianity: what was too Platonic to rest on the plain text of Scripture could always be extracted from an allegorical interpretation of it. The mediaeval Church had used its fourfold interpretation in similar fashion to bring in Aristotle. The result was that much of the fabric of mediaeval theology rested on interpretations of Scripture, some of which only a scholar, skilled in the application of typology and allegory, could comprehend. The plain man, uninstructed in these methods of interpretation, might well be led astray at certain points by the mere surface meaning of Scripture,

[1] Quoted by Dobschütz, *loc. cit.*   [2] Knox's *Works*, edit. Laing, Vol. IV, p. 137ff.

and might thereby err from the Catholic Truth, or even be led to doubt whether the Catholic Truth was God's truth.

The danger of such errors in Biblical interpretation was connected with an important change which had occurred in the meaning of the word "faith". In the Bible, faith does not mean primarily assent to dogma, but trustful self-commitment to the God who addresses us in Jesus Christ. Yet in such self-commitment there is always some element of intellectual assent: and for that reason, creeds and confessions are necessary evils. But every fresh credal formulation represents a temptation to change the emphasis from trust and personal commitment to intellectual assent to dogma: so that those who began by saying "Believe on the Lord Jesus Christ and thou shalt be saved", may finish up by saying "Assent to the propositions of the Nicene Creed, or thou shalt be damned."

By the time of Luther, his antagonist Tetzel had no difficulty in propounding more than threescore theological propositions, all allegedly distilled from Scripture by one means or another, denial of any one of which involved damnation. Faith had ceased to be trust: it had become acceptance of dogma.

It was this intellectualized conception of faith that made Bible reading appear to the Church a perilous business. By the innocent misunderstanding of some text, and quite unaware of his offence, the uninstructed layman might commit "a fatal error of belief", and be led by his study of the Bible, not to salvation but to perdition. Browning has hit off the attitude neatly in his *Soliloquy of the Spanish Cloister:*—

> There's a great text in Galatians,
>   Once you trip on it, entails
> Twenty-nine distinct damnations,
>   One sure, if another fails.

The Church believed, in all honesty, that the generality of men would be much safer to confine their reading to approved and orthodox literature, rather than venture to the perilous fountainhead of scalding hot truth. Biblical sanction for this attitude was found, by typical allegorizing and typology, in Exodus 19 :

Mount Sinai represents Scripture, and the layman who accidentally or presumptuously trespasses on the Holy Mount shall die.

It was this growing sense of the difficulty and danger of the Bible that produced the characteristic mediaeval shift of emphasis from the authority of Scripture to the authority of the Church.[1]

The change of emphasis was largely unconscious. The mediaeval Church believed wholeheartedly that its doctrines were Scriptural, and that Scripture was the supreme religious authority. But when Scripture had such a bewildering variety of senses— each text having a literal, a moral, an allegorical, and an anagogic meaning, and all of them different: when the truth was so hard to find, and error believed to be so perilous—it was obviously necessary for the Church to step in and to specify which particular interpretation of Scripture was to be regarded as the correct one. Inevitably this diminished the authority of Scripture and enhanced the authority of Church tradition.

The position was, of course, quite untenable: for if Scripture is the sole and final authority, the Church has no standing to guarantee or specify one particular interpretation as truth, and all rival interpretations as damning falsehoods; rather must the Church adopt an attitude of humble teachability, and of willingness to reconsider all its doctrines if new light should break forth from the Word. This, of course, was what the Reformers invited the Church to do, and set themselves to do in the Reformed Church —as witness the preamble to the *Scots Confession*.[2] But the mediaeval Church was precluded from any such course by its defective understanding of the Bible: if it once stepped away from the solid rock of Churchly authority, it could see no other solid ground anywhere, but only the shifting sands of wilder and still more wild private interpretations of Scripture. Eventually the great Reformation debates convinced the Roman Church of what it had not clearly realized before: that not all its doctrines and practices had

[1] "Whoever does not hold to the doctrine of the Roman Church and of the Roman Pontiff as an infallible rule of faith, from which even Holy Scripture draws its strength and authority, is a heretic." Prierias, *Dialogus de potestate Papae*, Fundamentum tertium.

[2] "If any man will note in this our Confession any article or sentence repugnant to God's holy Word ... we promise unto him ... reformation of that which he shall prove to be amiss."

33

Scriptural warrant. And at the Council of Trent, in the mid-sixteenth century, the Roman Church took the fateful—but on its own principles the inevitable—step of erecting Church tradition explicitly to a co-ordinate authority with Scripture; and implicitly, and by the logic of the situation, to a position of absolute superiority over Scripture. For it was now the Church that decided, by its own tradition, what Scripture should be permitted to mean.

This was the developing situation against which the Reformers reacted in formulating their teaching on Scripture; and Knox exhibits as clearly as any of them the fundamentals of the Reformed position.

The basic Reformed doctrine is that of the *perspicuitas* or intelligibility of Scripture to the ordinary pious mind. And this doctrine was never more trenchantly stated than by John Knox in his first interview with Mary Queen of Scots: "The word of God is plain in itself; and if there appear any obscurity in one place, the Holy Ghost, who is never contrary to Himself, explains the same more clearly in other places: so that there can remain no doubt, but to such as obstinately remain ignorant."[1]

Article 18 of the *Scots Confession* makes the same point in almost the same words, with the additional explanation that obscure passages are to be interpreted by reference to the general tenor of the revelation given in Scripture, and the warning that this comparison of Scripture with Scripture is much more important than the collation of the views of earlier commentators. One may compare Zwingli's remark: "I discovered that I must learn the meaning of the Word out of the Word itself: so I asked God to give me light, and then the Scriptures began to become much more intelligible when I read them, themselves, alone, than when I read much commentary and exposition."[2] Indeed, all the Reformers testify to the perspicuity of Scripture when read in its own light.

Along with this we may set Knox's advice in his *Letter of*

[1] Knox, *History*, Vol. 2, p. 18.
[2] Zwingli, *Works*, edit. Schuler and Schulthess, Vol. I, p. 79.

Wholesome Counsel of 1556[1]—to read widely, not in snippets of a few verses; but rather, if possible, whole books at a time. And to read, concurrently, a book of the Old with a book of the New Testament, noting what light one sheds upon the other; for (to quote his words) "it shall greatly comfort you to hear that harmony and well-tuned song of the Holy Spirit speaking in our fathers from the beginning ... and to behold the face of Christ Jesus his loving spouse and Church, from Abel to Himself, and from Himself to this day, in all ages to be one."

Here we have, admirably stated, the essentials of the Reformed doctrine of the *perspicuitas* of Scripture. The Bible is not a ragbag of assorted proof-texts, as the mediaeval Church had made it: it is a unity of revelation, and is to be read in the light of the revelation which it, itself, communicates. Take it where you will, it tells—chapter after chapter—the one story of God's unfolding plan of redemption. Isolated sentences, torn from their context, may well be unintelligible or even misleading; but their meaning will become plain when they are read as parts of the great story. Therefore read widely to learn the story, before reading narrowly to elucidate the meaning of single texts.

Knox never suggests that the services of the trained exegete and the theologian are unimportant. Quite the contrary. The *perspicuitas* of Scripture does not mean, as the Anabaptists imagined, that the man in the pew can dispense with the man in the pulpit, and un-riddle all Scripture with the sole assistance of the Holy Spirit. Knox is well aware that the ordinary believer may have neither the time nor the ability to reach that conspectus of all Scripture which is essential to a balanced interpretation of specific texts, or to the formulation of a body of doctrine. For the presentation of the Faith in its wholeness, for the well-being of the Church and of the individual believers who require to hear the Word in its wholeness for their edification in the faith, the labours of trained exegete, theologian, and skilled preacher are essential.

But the *perspicuitas* of Scripture did mean this: that the wayfaring men, though fools, would meet their God in the Bible,

[1] *Works*, IV, p. 133ff.

hear His voice, take His promises and comforts and rebukes personally and directly to themselves, and understand enough of what was being said to them to receive, by faith, salvation. And since faith means the personal commitment that follows this personal encounter with the God of the Bible, and does not mean assent to a body of doctrines, no man will be mortally harmed by incidental errors or deficiencies of belief—provided he is humble enough to learn better, when that which is better is clearly presented to him by those whose duty it is to shepherd him in the faith.

Knox's other qualification to the doctrine of perspicuity is also worthy of note: he makes it in his *Letter of Wholesome Counsel*.[1] The *perspicuitas* is not to be taken to mean that the profane man can read off the revelation of God from the Bible pages. The Bible is perspicuous to those (and only to those) who have dwelling in them that same Spirit who inspired the writers of Scripture. But the gift of the Spirit is not the dower of the specially holy or the specially clever, but dwells by faith in the heart of every believer— so that all who believe, hear the Word. The Holy Spirit inspired the Bible: if you have the Holy Spirit, you will understand it.

So Knox gave the Bible back to the people of Scotland; and gave it not merely by placing the book in their hands, but rather by supplying them with a key to its understanding, and practical guidance for their study of it.

There is a further aspect of Knox's instruction on Bible study which merits attention, the more so because little note is generally taken of it: and that is his emphasis on the necessity of group study. Private Bible study, and attendance at the public preaching of the Word, are essential: but Knox is quite clear that these are not enough—and the Church to-day would do well to heed his advice.

"Considering," he says in his *Letter of Wholesome Counsel*,[2] "that St Paul calleth the congregation 'the body of Christ', whereof every one of us is a member, teaching us thereby that no

[1] *Loc. cit.*   [2] *Loc. cit.*

member is of sufficiency to sustain and feed itself without the help and support of another; I think it necessary for the conference of Scriptures, that assemblies of brethren be had"—if possible once a week.

Directions are given for the conduct of these small study groups, in which every member is to be free to contribute to the common pool such understanding of Scripture as he has: or to seek aid in the solution of doubts and problems that perplex him. Knox is tremendously careful to insist that, in dealing with difficult texts, the group must never be content to let the matter rest in disagreement. No loophole is to be left for the divisive Anabaptist idea that the Holy Spirit may reveal one truth to one man in a certain text, and an entirely different truth to another—both truths being thus divinely guaranteed and therefore equally valid—and that that is the end of the matter, each man being left free to believe as the Spirit moves him. If that were so, we might as well throw the Bible in the fire and wait for our private revelations from heaven. But the revelation in Scripture is given in and through history, and is objective. The Bible says what it says, and means what it means, and it is the business of the group to find that meaning. If they cannot find it, they are to reduce their difficulty to writing, and seek the assistance of more expert exegetes. But, by one means or another, they are to work on the difficulty until the Word that is being spoken in Scripture becomes clear to them all.

These study groups persisted in Scotland. They did not vanish without remainder into "Presbyteries": they persisted at congregational level and they were still active in the opening years of the Covenanting struggle.[1] And I should say that it is largely to them, and to Knox's insistence on fighting through to an agreed understanding of Scripture, that Scotland owed its remarkable freedom from the early schisms that broke up the unity of the Reformed Church in other lands. And here also one might see the glimmering of a way towards Protestant reunion: that men of differing views should sit down, in honesty and humility of heart, not to argue about doctrine but to study the Bible together: and that

[1] See, for example, Burnet, *History of His own Time*, Bk. 2, p. 102.

they should refuse to give up until they have heard, all together, the Word and commandment of God which they must obey.

We pass to another aspect of Knox's view of Scripture—its authority. At this point Knox and the other early Reformers have been much misrepresented. Despite all that has been said and written to the contrary, these men did not proclaim the infallibility of Scripture as a counter-blast to the infallibility of the Pope. It was not the infallibility of Scripture that interested them, so much as its supreme authority; and that authority they proclaimed not as a matter of dogma, but as a matter of experience.

For the same experience had come to all these men. Luther in his spiritual distress reading Romans: Calvin the young humanist searching the New Testament for principles of morality: Knox reading the 17th chapter of John: to each of them, God had suddenly spoken from His Word. Each had felt himself to be personally addressed by God out of the pages of the Bible; had felt the Gospel of God's grace pressed directly upon his own heart and conscience. For each of them, this personal encounter with the God of the Bible was the ground and foundation of all Christian faith and knowledge. By the strength of it, and in the light of it, each man walked for the remainder of his life. "The Word of God," says Knox, "is the beginning of life spiritual; without which all flesh is dead in God's presence."[1] And by "Word of God" he does not mean the text of Scripture but the living word that comes into man's experience through Scripture.

God, then, speaks: and when man hears, he cannot but bow before the supreme authority of all. He needs no other authority to assure him of the divine authority. God is His own authority, and God's Spirit in the man's heart—the *testimonium internum Spiritus Sancti*—answers Amen to the voice that speaks through Scripture.

But the voice of God speaks a Word and a message: and that message is the Gospel of salvation through Jesus Christ. Thus, when a man hears the voice of God in Scripture, he is aware not

[1] *Works*, IV, p. 133.

only of the authority of the divine Voice that speaks, but aware of the authority, the compelling truth, the indubitability, the infallibility, of the message that is spoken. God's voice cannot speak error, but only truth. So the whole Gospel message contained in Scripture is invested with divine authority and truth. It no more needs to be established by papal or ecclesiastical testimonial than does the authority of God Himself. Once again, he who hears— really hears—this Word of the Gospel is assured of its truth and authority by the *testimonium internum Spiritus Sancti*. Hence the words of the *Scots Confession*: "We affirm and avow the authority of the Scriptures to be of God, and neither to depend on men or angels. We affirm, therefore, such as allege the Scripture to have no authority, but that which is received from the Church, to be blasphemous against God ..."[1]

It is worth observing that there is no necessary logical connexion between this Reformed assertion of the infallible truth of the Gospel given in and through Scripture, and the later doctrine of the verbal inerrancy of the Bible text. Luther certainly held no doctrine of verbal inerrancy, and neither did Calvin. Knox has left us little exegetical material by which we might judge of his views on this point; but from what he does say, I judge it to be unlikely that he would have committed himself to a doctrine of verbal inerrancy; though it must be admitted that in the heat of controversy he could (like St Paul) hang a whole volume of divinity on the turn of a Biblical phrase.

There was, however, in Knox's doctrine of Scripture one grave and unhappy shortcoming. As we have seen, he rightly discerned the important truth that Scripture is a unity of revelation—that the story of the divine plan and purpose of redemption links together the Old Testament and the New inseparably. What he failed to realize clearly was that, in addition to this continuity, the Bible also exhibits a terrific discontinuity: a discontinuity marked by the newness of all things in Christ.

Certainly Our Lord Himself stresses the continuity—"Think

[1] Cap. XIX.

not that I am come to destroy the Law, or the Prophets: I am not come to destroy, but to fulfil." Yes! But the fulfilment is such that it completely transforms what it fulfils; for Our Lord also said "Ye have heard that it hath been said by them of old time. ... But I say unto you ..." If that means anything to us, it must mean this: that the Old Testament must be baptized into Christ before it can be used for Christian edification and guidance.

Too often Knox failed to make this baptism—perhaps failed to realize that there was necessity for it. One finds him using a text (say) from the Book of Judges, as if it were on exactly the same footing as a saying of Christ in the Gospels. I am far from objecting to Knox's practice of extracting political theory from the Hebrew prophets: that is precisely the place it ought to be extracted from, and all politicians would be greatly benefited (or at any rate we who are ruled by them should be greatly benefited) if they would make a careful study of the Hebrew prophets. His use of the prophets, in this connexion, is entirely laudable: but his uncritical handling of other parts of the Old Testament such as the Book of Kings is rather frightening. Can it be right, for example, to hold up the doings of Jehu as worthy of emulation by some bold Christian Reformer who sees his brethren oppressed by a modern Jezebel? Bloody deeds can be given an aura of sanctity from the Scriptures by those who do not realize that a New Age begins with the advent of Christ, and that what was done by them of old time may be quite inexcusable in those who live on this side of Advent. Knox cannot be absolved from blame here; though he was no more guilty than many another of his time.

In thus handling Scripture, Knox was untrue to his own basic insights. For he had been called in, and by, the Gospel: and the Gospel was therefore his authority, and out of the spirit of the Gospel he had no warrant to go. Luther was wiser here, for he knew that the Gospel must ever be held above the Law, and he always read the Old Testament in the light of the New.

Yet, to be fair to Knox, his bark was usually much worse than his bite. And it is also a notable fact that there was infinitely more bloodshed and cruelty in Luther's Germany than in Knox's

Scotland; for although Luther held the Gospel above the Law, he also placed politics outside the sphere of the Gospel: so that while Christ was preached in the Church, He was denied by the state, and civil violence was unbridled by religion. This was an error Knox did not make.

It is indeed hard to say which is the worse—Knox's blessing of the sword, or Luther's denial of responsibility for its deeds. In the long run, Luther's is probably the more disastrous error.

But when all just criticisms have been passed, this remains— that Knox gave the Bible to Scotland, taught his countrymen to know and love it and to recognize in it that divine authority which is above all authorities on earth.

3

THE SACRAMENTS

3

The Sacraments

TO be invisible is a frustrating experience, and one that seems to afflict some of us pretty frequently in shops and public offices. We wait in growing exasperation while those who came in long after us are served before us. Not until everyone else has been attended to, and we are left alone at the counter, do we apparently click into focus; and then some assistant, with languidly raised eyebrows, comes out with the inevitable fatuous query: "Were you wanting something?"

It is always difficult, on the spur of the moment, to produce a wholly adequate reply to that question.

I had a similar experience some months ago, not in a shop but in my own study, when I consulted an article on the sacraments by an eminent Cambridge scholar. In it, the sacramental doctrines of Luther, Zwingli, Calvin, the Anglican Fathers, and the Anabaptists were sympathetically set out and fairly and adequately discussed. The present-day sacramental beliefs and practices of various modern denominations were reviewed, right down even to those which have none: the Quakers and the Salvation Army. English Presbyterianism and the Westminster Confession had a small but respectable paragraph to themselves. But in the sixteen pages of close-packed summary there was just one half-line devoted to the sacraments in the Scottish Church. It consisted of three pregnant words—"Scotland followed Calvin".

I have seldom felt a more exasperating and humiliating sense of invisibility. And I cannot accept the suggestion, no matter who makes it, that the teaching and practice of Knox, the testimony of the *Scots Confession*, and the distinctive sacramental emphasis of the Scottish Church through four centuries can be summed up in three words—"Scotland followed Calvin".

We may as well begin our discussion with a point made by the writer of the offending article. In attempting to exhibit the characteristic sacramental trend of Calvinism, the writer begins by quoting Calvin himself:—

"It is an error to suppose that anything more is conferred by the sacraments than is offered by the Word of God and obtained by true faith. ... Assurance of salvation does not depend on participation in the sacraments, as if justification consisted therein. This ... we know to be communicated not less by preaching of the Gospel than by the seal of a sacrament; and it may be completely enjoyed without this seal."[1]

Arguing that Calvin's attitude makes the sacraments simply an additional, but not strictly necessary, prop to weak faith, and must lower their value as compared with that of preaching, the writer goes on to say: "The Puritans wanted a lecture when Archbishop Laud wanted an altar: and the sermon holds the central place in the Church life of modern nonconformity which the Mass holds in the Roman Catholic Church."

I do not know whether English Nonconformists in general would accept this as a fair statement: some would certainly do so. But this cannot be recognized as a fair comment on Scottish sacramental belief or practice. No one who knows at all intimately the sentiments of a modern Scottish congregation, and no one who knows anything about the great, if infrequent, communion seasons of a bygone age in Scotland, could subscribe to the opinion that the sacraments have sunk to a merely secondary significance in the Scottish Church. We have never regarded Sermon and Sacrament as competitors for our esteem, so that if the one receives more of it, the other is bound to receive less. At the centre of Scottish Church life stand always these two things—not independent of one another, and certainly not competitive—but the Word and the Sacrament together. And the reverence which the Scottish Churchman feels for the preached Word of God is matched only by his deep sense of awe at the Sacrament of the Lord's Supper. I have taken the Lord's Supper in Churches of

[1] *Institutes* IV, xiv, 14.

various denominations in widely different parts of the world, and this has impressed me deeply: that in no place have I felt more of this deep, quiet, sense of awe before the mystery of the Sacrament than in the Scottish Church; and in few places have I felt so much. The Scottish Church has always been sacramental as well as evangelical.

As for Knox himself, I shall attempt to show that it was precisely in his teaching on the sacraments that he departed significantly from Calvin—closely though he followed him in most other things: and that for this reason it will not do to say that in matters sacramental "Scotland followed Calvin". This is the point at which Scotland significantly diverged.

Since Knox and his fellow-Reformers in Scotland defined their sacramental teaching in conscious opposition to the Roman, Zwinglian, and Anabaptist views, and since we shall be attempting to discuss Lutheran and Calvinist influences on it, we must look first at the Roman position and at the movements away from it in the various branches of the Reformation.

The mediaeval doctrine of the sacraments was based on two conceptions—or, as the Reformers contended, misconceptions—about Justification and Grace. The mediaeval Church believed that to "justify" means to "make just", to "make righteous". Thus when St Paul speaks of being justified before God, it was supposed that he meant that our salvation consists in being made righteous. To the mediaeval Church, therefore, Justification meant a gradual process taking place within the soul of man, whereby he is built up in holiness, and is finally presented faultless before the throne of God.

This process requires the full co-operation of the human will; but the human will alone is not sufficient to effect it. A man must first be set in the way of holiness by supernatural power; and by further periodic accessions of supernatural power he must be aided to persist therein, until his justification is completed, and he is fit for heaven. Grace was supposed, by the mediaeval Church, to be the supernatural power which man required periodically to

47

have infused into him. And the sacraments were conceived to be the channels through which this supernatural grace was infused into human nature. Two sacraments were felt to be scarcely sufficient to convey to man all the grace he needed to see him through life; and seven were, in fact, postulated.

Baptism, by applying the merits of the Sacrifice of Calvary, cancelled the guilt of original sin and left the soul innocent before God, with a clear road to salvation before it, provided no further sin was ever committed. Further sins, however, were always committed: and the Sacrament of Penance was then required to give renewed infusions of grace, and to restore the condition of baptismal innocence.

When we come to the Lord's Supper, we find that by the later mediaeval period it was not really one sacrament, but two. Granted the miracle of transubstantiation whereby the bread and wine became, in very substance, the Body and Blood of Christ, the Body and Blood could then be used in two quite distinct ways. They could be offered to men—as Communion: or they could be offered to God—as sacrifice.

When offered to men, they provided the supreme infusion of spiritual power: the divine substance entering into and vitalizing the human. When offered to God, they constituted the sacrifice of the mass. The mediaeval theologians could not agree about what the sacrifice of the mass meant; but the popular mind knew quite well what it meant. It meant that the sacrifice once made on Calvary was not enough to propitiate God for the constant sinfulness of men. It meant that unless the priest was constantly offering up the Body and Blood of Christ on the altar, there could be no forgiveness or salvation for anybody.

It was, of course, in relation to this sacrament that the power of the priest reached its climax. For, without him, the bread and wine remained mere bread and wine; and man was left with no means of union with Christ, and no sacrifice to appease the wrath of God.

It will be observed that, in all this system, the Word of God is decidedly peripheral. Study of Scripture, preaching, the hearing and intelligent comprehension of the Gospel, are of secondary importance. It is the sacraments, as the channels to man of supernatural grace, that are the central things—the things that really save. At a pinch you can do without the Word (and many a Scottish parish had to do without it for years at a stretch before the Reformation) but you can do nothing without the sacraments with their infusions of supernatural grace.

The Reformers, by restoring the New Testament meanings of the words "Justification" and "Grace", transformed the whole theological landscape. All the old landmarks vanished, and a theological re-survey and re-mapping of sacramental doctrine was forced upon them. Certain doctrines were common to all the Reformers: but as they approached their enormous (and still unfinished) task from different angles, and were often preoccupied with different practical problems, divergences of emphasis were inevitable. These, hardening into dogma, produced the tragic sacramental divisions of the non-Roman Churches.

Taking first the doctrines held in common, we find that the Reformers think of grace as primarily the gracious attitude of God towards sinners, and not as a supernatural quality that requires to be infused into man.

Justification, also, is not a process taking place in man: it is the act in which God, out of His pure grace, acquits sinners of all guilt before Him, on account of the sacrifice of Christ on Calvary. This state of justification is initiated and continued by God's pure graciousness: there is therefore no need of infusions of grace into man, in order to maintain an attitude which is in God.

Immediately we say this, the sacraments lose their sole centrality. For what comes to man now for his salvation is not an infusion of grace at all, but a message—a Gospel—a Word of Salvation. What man needs, now, is to hear this Word, and to grasp it for himself by faith—which faith is quickened in him by the Holy Spirit. And this conviction of unmerited forgiveness, of God's love, of Christ's passion and sacrifice, is in itself so transforming

49

that it initiates (and, being constantly renewed, sustains) his growth in holiness.

It follows that the sacraments must now be defined by their relationship to the Word. Apart from it, they mean nothing, effect nothing, convey nothing.

This means that they can no longer be the centre-point of the Church's life. They must either share that centrality with the Word: or the Word must become central, and the sacraments secondary and peripheral. Different branches of the Reformation gave different answers to this alternative: it depended on whether the sacraments were held to be as essential to the true reception of the Word, as the Word was essential to the true reception of the sacraments—or whether the Word was conceived as self-sufficient, or at least requiring only a certain amount of aid from the sacraments for its more effectual working.

This issue was unfortunately cut across and confused for the Reformers by the necessity of a polemic against the mass. The mass had to be demolished: first, because it was the citadel of priestly power by which Rome stood or fell; second, because it suggested that the sacrifice on Calvary had not been sufficient, when the essence of the Gospel was just that it had been, is, and will be, all-sufficient for man's salvation; third, because by pretending to offer the Body and Blood of Christ to propitiate the wrath of God, it exactly reversed the true meaning of both the Sacrament and the Word—which is that God offers the Body and Blood to us to assure us that He has been forever propitiated, and that all His thoughts towards us are mercy and love.

The quick way to demolish the mass was to deny transubstantiation, and this all the Reforms did, thereby ruling out a priestly sacrifice of the Body and Blood to God. But this left the Reformers to decide just what they understood the bread and wine to be, or signify. And on this narrower question they stuck and altercated, without fully clearing up the major question of the relation of Word and Sacrament.

Luther's attitude was that, in receiving Christ in the Sacrament, the soul is finally assured that the Gospel Word of reconciliation is true, and real, and is offered and applied to it. Without this personal reception of Christ in the Sacrament, our faith would hang in the air. Thus his attitude is really that Word and Sacrament are "co-central".[1]

To secure this reception of Christ in the Sacrament, so essential to an assured faith in the Gospel, Luther formulated his doctrine of consubstantiation—of the material or substantial presence of the Body and Blood in the bread and wine, though not by priestly miracle.

Zwingli was not concerned to deny what Luther held dear— the reception of Christ in the Sacrament. But consubstantiation, and the idea that Christ could be received by the mouth, seemed to him both ridiculous and blasphemous. The reception can only be spiritual, and it can only be by faith. The bread and wine must be regarded as signs representing the sacrifice on Calvary, so that our faith and love, being stirred up thereby, may rise to an apprehension of the living and glorified Christ.

Plainly, the sacraments are more peripheral for Zwingli: they are aids and stimuli to the faith that spiritually apprehends Christ; but the faith is there without the sacraments, and the spiritual apprehension is there without the sacraments. They help, but they are scarcely essential.

The Anabaptists pressed far beyond Zwingli in rationalization of the sacraments. There was no mystery or mystic union in them. They were merely symbolic or pictorial statements of Scripture truth—dramatized sermons: and their effect was in no respect different from that of a good sermon in bringing home to mind and heart the Gospel, as the Anabaptists understood it. Here the sacraments have undoubtedly become peripheral: the Word is everything. And it is but a step to the position of the Quakers who hold that a stout faith really does better without these external dramatic representations of doctrine.

Calvin, coming half a generation after Luther and Zwingli, is generally described as holding a central position between them.

---

[1] In his *Treatise on N.T.*, however, Luther regards the Word alone as being absolutely necessary to salvation: the sacraments have only a relative necessity. "One might be saved without sacrament, yet not without testament."

Certainly the Zwinglians moved into agreement with him: and Luther, though by no means satisfied that all the barriers were down, was attracted to, and impressed by, Calvin's teaching on the sacraments.

My own rash opinion (I am aware that it is rashness in a historian to do other than tread with nervous circumspection in the tricky territory of theology) is that Calvin's position looks central because he is, as usual, inconsistent: or perhaps I should rather say that he has one doctrine which is indeed a central position; but that he makes a good many statements which appear to me to be incompatible with it, and to be anything but "central".

His interest was to secure in the Sacrament, like Luther, union with Christ—but Christ risen, living and glorified, and seated at the right hand of God. Christ's body no longer exists as a physical substance in this world: and if it did, what conceivable use would it be to us? Roman transubstantiation and Lutheran consubstantiation are therefore useless doctrines. It is not the substance of His body that we need, but the power of it. And that power we can have; for Christ is able to be present truly, really, with all His powers, where He pleases: and He pleases to be supremely thus present in the Sacrament, and through the bread and wine.

The bread and wine are therefore not mere tokens of the body that was broken on Calvary long ago. They are the instruments of the glorious body that is at the right hand of God: and, through the bread and wine, all the life and power and immortality of that Body are made present to us, and active for us. So the bread and wine are truly, for us, His body and blood: or we can put it another way and say that they are sacramentally, not materially, His body and blood.

I think this means, as Luther also means, that Word and Sacrament are "co-central". Inevitably, and rightly, Calvin goes on to stress the Reformed position—that without the Word, the Sacrament would be nothing. To what end would bread and wine be held out to us, if the Word had not already held out to us Christ, by faith, to be our redeemer? We must believe, or we cannot receive. The Sacrament seals to us the proclamation and message of the Word.

If Calvin stopped there, he could not be reproached with inconsistency; but he does not stop there. Having used the most exalted language to describe the high mystery of the Eucharist,[1] he proceeds to a series of statements which appear to derogate gravely from this exalted view. Not content to call the sacraments seals, he can—in a polemical passage against Roman doctrine—describe them as *merely* seals. And in his treatment of Baptism he stresses that "the sacrament is afterwards added, as a kind of seal, not to give efficacy to the Promise, as if that were by itself not efficacious, *but merely to confirm it to us.*"[2]

Calvin's whole treatment of the sacraments exhibits a vacillation between a "high" doctrine and a merely "obsignatorial" one. There is clear inconsistency between his description of the Eucharist as a great mystery—a communion in the Body and Blood of Christ, and his description of it as a mere seal, a useful but not essential stimulus to faith.

This, however, is not all. Deeds speak louder than words. Despite his stress on the importance of weekly Communion, it is a curious fact that Calvin discouraged the persecuted Huguenots of France from seeking to institute the celebration of the sacraments: for the celebration of these could very well wait until such time as they had opportunity to organize their Church in an orderly manner.[3]

When Calvin takes the extremer form of his "obsignatorial" view, it is clear that the sacraments become peripheral; and that it is the Word alone—not the unity of Word and Sacrament—that he regards as central in the Church's life. I do not doubt him when he says that the individual Christian, in case of necessity, can survive without the sacraments; but I do doubt if the Church can exist without them. And if the Church cannot exist without them, they are not peripheral; and any theory of them that makes them appear so must be inadequate.

[1] E.g. in *Institutes* IV, xvii, 7, 32.   [2] *Institutes* IV, xv, 22.
[3] On this point see also *Institutes* IV, xv, 22, concluding sentences.

When we turn to a consideration of Knox's sacramental doctrine, we naturally have in mind the fact that like most Scots who were turning towards Reform, his early steps must have been guided (in part at least) by the writings of Martin Luther. In St Andrews Castle he was in the company of Balnaves, who had been deeply influenced by Luther: and in their subsequent captivity he co-operated with Balnaves in the production of a treatise on Justification which—as Professor Hugh Watt has conclusively shown—rests on Luther's Commentary on Galatians.

Now, if Luther's specifically sacramental teaching had made any impression on Knox, we should expect to find evidence of it in the first Communion Service he celebrated—probably in the Castle Chapel—at St Andrews. For our knowledge of that first Communion we depend on Knox himself, writing years later: and Knox, years later, is convinced that he had celebrated then exactly as he celebrates now, "in the same purity that now is ministered in the churches of Scotland, with that same doctrine."[1] Thus, if Knox's memory is to be trusted, he never was a Lutheran in sacramental doctrine or practice: and when we consider that Calvin's *Institutes* had been in print for some ten years before that St Andrews Communion, we realize that Knox had had the opportunity, by 1547, of becoming well acquainted with Calvin's teaching on the sacraments.

There is an additional piece of evidence bearing on that St Andrews Communion. Sir James Balfour had been one of the Castle garrison, and had attended Knox's Communion there. But when Knox was writing the first Book of his History, he notes[2] that the same Sir James had now withdrawn from the Communion of the Reformed Church—alleging, in justification of his action, that he had never been a Reformed Churchman: that having been brought up to hold Luther's doctrine of the sacraments, he could not now communicate under the Reformed rite.

Had Balfour been a man noted for consistency, this would have been good evidence that the Communion in St Andrews Castle had been more Lutheran than Knox remembered it to have been.

---

[1] Knox, *History*, I, p. 93.　　[2] *Loc. cit.*

But Balfour was a notorious time-server who would gladly have participated in a Witch's Sabbath if it would have got him anywhere. And Knox is undoubtedly right in saying that Balfour's only reason for withdrawing from Reformed Communion was that a gentleman hoping for advancement under Mary Queen of Scots was better not to be too closely identified with the Reformed Church—though for prudential reasons he was better to stop short of being an open Romanist.

All we can say, therefore, is that if Knox's memory is to be trusted, that first Communion in St Andrews was not explicitly Lutheran in form or doctrine, and may have been Calvinist.

We may add this small piece of supporting evidence. In 1550 Adam Wallace, Knox's successor as tutor at Ormiston, was martyred. And, if Foxe's account[1] is correct, Wallace at his trial rejected Luther's sacramental doctrine along with the Romanist doctrine, making the Calvinist avowal that the Body of Christ is at God's right hand and not in the bread and wine.

There is, therefore, no evidence that an explicitly Lutheran Communion was ever celebrated in Scotland, and a good deal of evidence that the earliest celebrations were more or less Calvinist in doctrine. Certainly, when Knox appears in England, it is the Calvinist rite and doctrine that he follows.

Yet there is ample evidence that, though Knox followed Calvin's doctrine on the sacraments, it was with some change of emphasis, and a very remarkable change of practice.

Calvin, as we have seen, though he held a high and mystical conception of the Communion, did not consider it to be absolutely essential to the life of the Church. Where Protestantism was persecuted and disorganized—where orderly discipline was impossible—it was better to postpone the institution of the sacraments. They belonged to the full life of the organized Church. Where the organized Church did not yet exist, individual piety would not be hurt by their absence, nor would unbaptized infants suffer in any way: if elect, they were sure of salvation, whether baptized or not.

---

[1] *Acts and Monuments*, v, 636–641.

Knox's attitude was utterly different on this practical point, as we can learn from his practice during his visit to Scotland in 1555–56,[1] and again from his Mission to Kyle in 1562. During both missions, his practice was at every possible opportunity to gather the faithful into the drawing room of some gentleman's house, or some other convenient place, and there to administer the Sacrament of the Lord's Supper. There was no question of waiting for the establishment of an organized Church. Wherever two or three could be gathered together, there Knox administered Communion, carefully noting the date and place of celebration as important and significant events. The inference is clear: the Sacrament had an importance and a vital quality to Knox, that it apparently did not have to Calvin.

The reason for his attitude and practice may be seen in the little summary of sacramental doctrine, probably presented by him to the Council of the North when he was summoned to stand trial before them in 1550, during his ministry in the North of England.

In this little document,[2] in a remarkable and striking way, the whole action of the Sacrament is referred to Christ. There is nothing at all about what "we" do, or what the Church does. The Sacrament is not looked on as a ministerial act, or a Churchly ordinance. It is, first and last, something that Christ does for us. "The Lord Jesus, by earthly and visible things set before us, lifteth us up to heavenly and invisible things—He prepares His spiritual banquet—He witnesses that He Himself was the living bread—He sets forth the bread and wine to eat and drink—He giveth unto us Himself—and all this He does through the power of the Holy Ghost."

And then comes what I consider to be very significant: "Herewith, also, the Lord Jesus gathers us unto one visible body, so that we be members one of another, and make altogether one body, whereof Jesus Christ is the only Head."

This means, if words mean anything, not just that Christ gathers and creates the Church, but that He gathers it by this

---

[1] *History*, I, p. 121f. See also Percy, *John Knox*, p. 230f.   [2] *Works*, III, p. 73ff.

sacrament, and that on this sacrament He founds it. It is, says Knox, by this sacrament that He gathers us unto one visible body. It is by this sacrament that He makes us members one of another. It is by this sacrament that we are all made one body, with Christ the only Head.

I know nothing quite like this anywhere else in Reformed teaching. This is not a dispensable sacrament that Knox is describing; not one that may be postponed without serious harm until the visible body of the Church has been organized. This sacrament, as Knox describes it, is the very foundation of the visible body of the Church: by it, Christ brings that visible body into being. The Church is founded on the Word—yes: but on the Word completed and fulfilled by the action of Christ in the Sacrament.

Now, here is the reason why Knox, unlike Calvin, will not wait to celebrate the sacraments till the Church be formed; for it is the sacraments that form the Church. This is why Knox, in his missions in Scotland, gathers his two or three where he can, for the Lord's Supper. It is in these sacramental gatherings that they cease to be scattered believers, and begin to form "the face of a Kirk." Here they are made members one of another; here they are gathered by Christ Himself into one visible body, with Himself as Head. By Word and Sacrament the Church is created. On Word and Sacrament the Church is founded. But by Word alone, without Sacrament, the Church cannot be. To Knox, the Sacrament is creative, and basic, for the life of the Church, in a way it is not for Calvin—or anywhere else in the Reformed world. I should except not even Luther from this judgment; for though the Sacrament was so vital to Luther, it was so as a matter, primarily, of personal piety. None in the Reformed world made the Sacrament basic for the Church itself, as Knox did.

This emphasis has been permanent. It can be seen in the conventicle communions of the Covenanters, and in the great Communion gatherings of later times—and still in the Highland gatherings at Communion seasons. To the Scot, still, the centre of the Church's life is the solemn gathering at the Lord's Table where, after the Word, the Supper is dispensed. Percy, in his Life of Knox, has accurately noted this, and his words are worthy of quotation:—"Knox's conception of the central act of Christian worship set a lasting seal upon the Church of Scotland, differentiating it from all other Protestant Communions and making it, in the strict sense of the term, a Eucharistic church. His political vehemencies, systematized by others to conclusions his hot-headedness had never drawn, were to torture the body of Scotland for a century; but his vision of this one central truth was to save her soul."[1]

When we turn to the *Scots Confession*,[2] we find a position again resembling that of Calvin but again stated with a power and passion that remind one of Luther, and again stated in such a way that, while the doctrines of Calvin are followed, the emphasis and emotional tone are significantly altered.

There is a vehement repudiation, twice repeated, of Zwinglianism: "we utterly condemn the vanity of those that affirm Sacraments to be nothing else but naked and bare signs." Luther's consubstantiation is also, by implication, repudiated, and Calvin's point is emphasized against it: that there is "a far distance in place between His body now glorified in Heaven, and us now mortal in this earth."

But the dynamic presence of Christ—His body and blood—in the Sacrament (the teaching which was Calvin's great contribution to Reformed doctrine) is stated with glowing earnestness: indeed with such earnestness that it passes over into something more than Calvin's Calvinism, and certainly more than the Calvinism of any of Calvin's successors elsewhere than in Scotland. "We most assuredly believe that the bread which we break is the communion of Christ's body, and the cup we bless is the communion of His blood. We confess and undoubtedly believe that the faithful, in the right use of the Lord's Table, so do eat the body and drink the blood of the Lord Jesus, that He remaineth in them and they in Him; yea that they are so made flesh of His flesh

[1] Percy, *John Knox*, p. 65.
[2] *Scots Confession*, Cap. XXI. The *Confession* is printed as an appendix to Vol. 2 of Dickinson's edition of Knox's *History*: also in *Works* II, p. 113.

and bone of His bones, that, as the Eternal Godhead hath given to the flesh of Christ Jesus (which in its own condition and nature was mortal and corruptible) life and immortality; so doth Christ Jesus, His flesh and blood, eaten and drunken by us, give to us the same prerogative."

After cautioning us that these blessings are not given to us by the Sacrament apart from the Word, and that the blessings are not necessarily tied to the moment of participation in the Sacrament, the Confession goes on: "Yet we affirm that the faithful, in the right use of the Lord's Table, have such conjunction with Christ Jesus as the natural man cannot comprehend"—which reminds us of Calvin's remark: "It is too high a mystery either for my mind to comprehend, or my words to express ... I feel it, rather than understand it."[1]

The section closes with another reference to the Communion elements. "Liberally and frankly we must confess that we make a distinction betwixt Christ Jesus in His natural substance, and the elements in the sacramental signs; so that we will neither worship the signs in place of the thing which is signified by them, nor yet do we despise and interpret them as unprofitable and vain; but we use them with all reverence ..."

I think we may sum up by saying that Knox, and the *Scots Confession*, start with Calvin at his best, and go beyond him to something still better; and that never do they descend to the bareness of some of his obsignatorial utterances. I hope at any rate that I have demonstrated that it is impossible to rest content with the off-hand remark, "Scotland followed Calvin".

I should like, in closing, to refer briefly to the close link between the Lord's Supper and Ecclesiastical Discipline, which appears to be little understood.[2] The discipline which the Reformed Church insisted upon exercising was in no sense whatever an expression of legalism. It had nothing to do with legalism, or with any idea that God would be pleased with strict adherence to rules and regulations. Nor was it an expression of over-scrupulous moralism. Its

---

[1] *Institutes* IV, xvii, 32.   [2] See *Institutes* IV, xii, 5.

basis was this sense of the "numinous", or the "altogether holy", in the Lord's Supper—and the deep conviction that this holiness must not be profaned[1] by allowing the careless or the deliberately wicked to approach the Holy Table, at the sacred moment when the Lord and the participants were (as Knox put it) "knitted together".

Such scandalous persons must be exhorted to repent, and remedial discipline must be applied in the hope that they might be led to a better frame of mind. If this failed, they must be debarred, until they repented, from presenting themselves at the Lord's Table. This exclusion from the Sacrament—remedial, and it was to be hoped temporary—was what Knox understood by "excommunication". Knox's excommunication had nothing to do with consigning a soul to eternal damnation: it, and the whole discipline of the Kirk, were directed to one end—the protection of this central element of the Church's life from profanation.

One further misunderstanding must be dealt with. Knox had no use for a Pharisaic attitude among those who were admitted to Communion. All that he asked for was a repentant heart. Again and again he proclaimed that the Sacrament was "a singular medicine for all poor, sick, souls." Where else should the sinner go, but to the Good Physician? The Lord's Table was no place for those who trusted in themselves that they were righteous, any more than it was a place for the wilfully wicked, or the contemptuously indifferent. For, as Knox puts it in his Liturgy, "I seclude not any penitent person, howsoever grievous his sins have been, provided he feels in his heart unfeigned repentance for the same; but only such as continue in sin without repentance. ... Our Lord requireth no other worthiness on our part, but that we acknowledge our naughtiness and imperfection. ... For the end of our coming thither is not to make protestation that we are upright and just in our lives, but contrariwise, we come to seek our life and perfection in Jesus Christ."[2]

[1] A memorandum by the ministers of Geneva in 1537 has these words: "... que ceste Sainct Cène, instituée pour conjoindre les membres de Jésu-Crist avecq leur chefz ... ne soit souillée et contaminée ..."
[2] *Works*, VI, p. 324; IV, p. 193.

4

PREDESTINATION

4

Predestination

THERE are certain historical facts that are known to everybody: as, for example, that the Norman Conquest dated from 1066, and that Calvinism was a predestinarian faith. One might go further and say that everyone is aware that Calvinism was not only predestinarian, but adjectivally predestinarian—sternly, crudely, harshly predestinarian, and so on.

The main use of adjectives of this type is to induce the reader or hearer to pass judgment on purely emotional grounds, without asking to see the facts; thereby saving trouble all round, and producing the desired result more rapidly and certainly than argument and explanation could do it. For, of course, if a thing is stern, crude or harsh, it must be wrong; and we need think no more about it.

A wise man is instantly on the alert when he comes across such damnatory epithets. They may express an honest indignation: more often they indicate a desire to communicate an irrational dislike.

When applied to the Calvinist doctrine of predestination, these unpleasant adjectives are usually appeals to irrational emotion: for the most that the majority of those who use them know about predestination is the rather vague impression that it means that the good will go to Heaven no matter how naughty they are, while the bad will be damned no matter how well they behave. And I do not think that John Knox would recognize this as an adequate statement of his faith, or that anyone who reads what he has written on the subject would think so either.

Adjectives therefore, however colourful, will not excuse us from the task of acquainting ourselves with Knox's views. And that will be no easy task. For although Knox has left us a long treatment of the subject,[1] it is far from being a systematic one. It is a reply to an Anabaptist who had published an attack on Calvin's teaching on predestination; and instead of developing his own argument in an orderly way, Knox assails the Anabaptist's book, chapter by chapter, with all the ammunition he can lay his hands on. The result is much repetition, and repetition that is by no means always consistent with itself; so that it is often difficult to decide what is Knox's true view.

One has to bear in mind also that Knox was passionate and excitable, and that in the heat of debate he could be carried away to extremes to which, in his calmer moments, he was perhaps not prepared to commit himself.

And there is this further possible complication, that Knox's head may have been somewhat at variance with his heart. Intellectually, he was captivated by the theology of Calvin—as well he might be. But when he speaks and writes strictly as a pastor, one hears rather the voice of Martin Luther. I do not think that he was particularly interested in systematic theology, but rather in its pastoral and homiletic applications. For these reasons, I should be a little hesitant about assuming that the reply to the Anabaptist can be taken as representing Knox's own inmost convictions, or as the teaching that he communicated to his congregations. One has to weigh against it, rather carefully, references to predestination in his pastoral letters and elsewhere. Incidentally I must dissent from Percy's judgment that Knox was no pastor, and did not care for pastoral work.[2] His letters seem to me to reveal a man who was a pastor first, last, and all the time.

I am all the more inclined to doubt whether logical consistency is to be looked for in Knox's Treatise on Predestination, by the fact that in it he was following Calvin; and Calvin laid little store by logical consistency on this, or indeed on any other subject related to faith. We constantly hear references, of course, to Calvin's "ruthless (another damnatory adjective!) French logic",

---

[1] This treatise on Predestination occupies the greater part of Vol. V of his *Works*.
[2] *John Knox*, p. 59.

which pushed principles to their ultimate uncomfortable conclusions, without leaving any of these blurred edges or woolly compromises which, to the British mind, are infallible guarantees of balanced commonsense. One suspects that those who thus judge have been misled, by the limpid clarity and meticulous orderliness of Calvin's literary style, into supposing that the thought which it expresses is just as pellucid and neatly logical. This is not so, as anyone who tries to make a *précis* of his theology will quickly discover. His aim was to expound the truths of Biblical faith, as he understood them, without distortion: and he will not distort them, even in the interests of logical consistency. Again and again we are confronted with unresolved antinomy and paradox. Thus, after a lucid exposition of the majesty and sole sovereignty of God, he will proceed to stress the terrible reality and power of evil; not in order to offer any neat logical solution of the antinomy, for he has no such thing to offer—but simply because both sides of the antinomy are facts of Biblical witness, and of Christian faith and experience; and both, therefore, require the clearest statement that can be given them. A logical thinker would blur both sides of the antinomy in an effort to reach some sort of rational reconciliation between them, paring away something of the sovereignty of God, and something of the reality of evil;—until, with a limited God on the one hand, and evil that is not really evil but rather undeveloped good on the other, he could build some kind of logical bridge between the two. Calvin does no such thing. He states both sides of the antinomy with extreme sharpness, because both are, to him, incontrovertible facts which must not be minimized in any way, though they cannot be reconciled by logic. Truth, not logic, is his aim.

His treatment of Predestination is similar. On the one hand, he insists on outright and extreme predestination. On the other hand, no theologian ever put greater stress on human responsibility, and the importance and reality of human choice and decision, than Calvin. He states both sides without compromise or dilution, because he believes that both are *facts* which we dare not minimize or ignore; though how we are to reconcile them is an absolute mystery. We may call Calvin an extreme thinker if we like, provided we remember that his extremes are usually balanced by opposite extremes. He never nibbles the sharp edges off what he takes to be the facts. But the last thing we can accuse him of is "ruthless logic". It is the woolly-minded harmonizer who is really the ruthless logician—ruthless, all too often, with inconvenient facts and truths.

In his Treatise on Predestination, Knox is following Calvin's arguments pretty closely; and not only his arguments, but his methods also. Knox presents us with the same sharp statement of apparent contradictories. It would be a cheap victory, and a useless one, to rake out the numerous inconsistencies in his treatise. Knox would reply, like Calvin, that his aim was to state facts as he knew them to be, not to explain how they could be what they were. And, if it would be cheap simply to parade Knox's inconsistencies, it would be downright dishonest to label him as an "extremist" for his uncompromising assertion of one side of an antinomy, without pointing out that in the very next chapter he probably is just as extreme in his statement of the opposite truth. Indeed, Knox's views on Predestination are a balance of opposite extremes; a fact which the careless and hurried reader of his work is apt to miss.

There has been so much denunciation of the "ugly predestinarianism" of Calvinism and of John Knox—particularly on the part of some Scottish literary writers whose itch to pontify on theology seems scarcely to be warranted by the apparent sketchiness of their acquaintance with the subject[1]—that it seems to be altogether necessary to point out that neither Calvin nor Knox invented the doctrine, nor is it by any means peculiar to them.

The doctrine is Biblical. And it is Biblical not only in the sense that a Biblical basis can be found for it in certain utterances of St Paul, and of the prophets Isaiah and Jeremiah. The truth is

---

[1] A recent substantial work of literary criticism contains the statement that the cruel doctrine of the damnation of unbaptized infants was brought to Scotland from Geneva by John Knox! Can theological absurdity and misrepresentation go further? Probably it can, and will.

(and it was the merit of Calvin and of Knox after him that they realized this) *that the Bible is a book about predestination*. Predestination is its theme from start to finish. If the attempt is made to purge predestination from the pages of the Bible, what remains falls to pieces and loses significance, just as a beautiful necklace falls to meaningless bits and pieces when the string is withdrawn.

Consider how predestinarian the Bible is. In the Old Testament God is represented as sovereign in nature and in grace. His name is "I am", and He is God, and beside Him there is none other. His sovereign will, and only His will, ordains what is and what shall be. He created the world, down to its last detail; and He maintains it, down to its smallest event. Each morning He appoints to the sun its daily course, and each evening He brings out the stars by their number. The beasts of the forest receive their meat in due season from His hand; and when it is His pleasure to take away their breath, they die and return to the dust from which He created them. All nature, in all its details, is subject to His will; and all events come about as He ordains.[1]

Man, too, lives out his life in the hollow of God's hand, and the issues of that life lie with God's sovereign will. There is no escaping that divine surveillance which is so magnificently described in the 139th Psalm: "Thou knowest my very thoughts from afar ... and before ever a word comes to my tongue, Thou knowest it altogether. Thou art on every side, behind and before, and layest Thy hand on me. ... If I take the wings of the morning and dwell in the uttermost parts of the sea, even there would Thy hand reach me, and Thy right hand would grasp me." But the Psalmist is sure not only of God's ordaining of all his life, but of His foreordaining of it: "All the days of my life were foreseen by Thee, set down within Thy book; ere ever they took shape, they were assigned me, ere ever one of them was mine."[2]

Here indeed is predestination! In the Old Testament—if we except the cynicism of Ecclesiastes—there is no such thing as chance or fate. All things fall out by the sovereign will and

---

[1] See Psalm 104.   [2] Moffatt's translation.

determination of God. And, since He sees the end from the
beginning, not just by His determination but by His pre-deter-
mination or predestination. Not even evil is excepted from this
sovereign determination of God—and this despite the constant
stress upon His holiness and goodness: "Shall there be evil in a
city, and the Lord hath not done it?[1]" "I make peace, and create
evil: I the Lord do all these things."[2]

As in the realm of nature, so also in the realm of grace: God
chose Israel when Israel was nothing, and of sheer grace, and of
His own good pleasure, elected Israel to be His chosen people and
the instruments of His purposes of blessing. The destiny of the
nation was determined by God, not for any special qualities which
Israel had, for God gave all these qualities subsequently to His
choice. The choice of God determined in all details the destiny of
the people: it was a pre-destination.[3]

The New Testament, too, is saturated with Predestination. In
the fulness of time—at the appointed and determined hour—God
sent His Son, and sent Him to do a pre-determined work. The
events of His life fell out "that it might be fulfilled which was
spoken by the prophets." As He faced death, Our Lord exclaimed
"For this cause came I unto this hour." And to the disciples on the
Emmaus journey He said "O fools and slow of heart to believe
all that the prophets have spoken: ought not Christ to have
suffered these things, and afterwards to enter into His glory"—
was not this the role appointed and fore-ordained for Him by
God?

As the Lord's destiny was fore-ordained, so was the disciples'.
"I have manifested Thy Name," says Christ in His High Priestly
prayer, "to the men Thou gavest me out of the world. Thine they
were, and Thou gavest them to me ... Thou hast given Thy son
power over all flesh, that He should give eternal life to as many
as Thou hast given him." They did not choose; they were chosen.
These last words come (significantly) from that 17th chapter of
St John's Gospel where Knox said that he "cast his first anchor".

[1] Amos 3 : 6.   [2] Isaiah 45 : 7.   [3] Cf. Leviticus 20 : 26.

Who could cast anchor there, and not be a predestinarian out and out?

And finally, the end to which all the processes of nature and grace are moving—the final consummation—is hidden in the determinate foreknowledge of God. "Of that day and hour knoweth no man, no, not the angels of heaven, but my Father only."

Surely enough evidence has now been adduced to show that the doctrine of Predestination does not rest precariously on a few doubtful proof-texts. Predestination is what the Bible is about, and no theology can claim to be Biblical which is not strung on this same predestinarian thread.

It is unnecessary, therefore, to apologize for the predestinarian strain in Knox's theology. It was his business to expound the Biblical faith, and the Biblical faith is predestinarian from end to end. It is those who object to his predestinarian teaching who must show how it can be rejected without rejecting the Bible as well.

What can be questioned, however, is whether certain emphases in Knox's handling of the doctrine give a really balanced presentation of this fundamental element of the Biblical testimony.

One question suggests itself immediately. If all the Reformers were thorough predestinarians (as indeed they were) why does Calvinism have the reputation of being an ultra-predestinarian creed? The main reason is that Calvin's theological interests, and therefore his dogmatic formulations, range over a wider field than Luther's, so that there is more for him to be predestinarian about. Luther was a monk and an anti-humanist with a strong distaste for speculation: his interest was practical, and was focused to one burning point—man's sin and need, and what God has done to meet that need. At that point he is, of course, predestinarian; perhaps even more completely so than Calvin. On the wider fields of theology, however—especially where it borders on speculation and philosophy—Luther has, comparatively speaking, less to say. His predestinarianism is therefore displayed on a fairly narrow front.

Calvin, on the other hand, was a converted humanist—yet a

humanist still with wide-ranging interests. He begins his theology, not at the subjective point of sinful man's predicament, but with God in His infinite glory and sovereignty; and from this he passes down through the whole range of the divine creation and scheme of redemption before reaching the application of that redemption to the individual sinner. His method of thought thus compels him to present predestination over a far wider front than Luther did: and it is the wide range of his predestinarianism, corresponding to the wide range of his theology, that is the main cause of the general impression that Calvinism is abnormally predestinarian.

In his Treatise on Predestination, however, Knox follows Luther's method rather than Calvin's: that is to say, he begins from predestination as it bears directly on our own personal salvation. From that central point he makes excursions into the wider field of Christian philosophy, and back towards those eternal decrees of God on which predestination is conceived to be founded. His chief interest is in the relation between God's foreordination and our salvation, and the topics that take up his attention are those of election and reprobation, the nature of human responsibility, the problem of assurance and of the perseverance of the saints, and the relationship between election and the mediation of Christ.

Knox begins, as do all the Reformers, with the assertion that salvation is altogether of God's grace, and rests not in the smallest measure on our good works. He grounds this assertion not only on the fact that sinful man cannot produce good works with which to justify himself before God, but must ever be a debtor to God's mercy and grace—Luther's starting-point: much more does Knox found himself on the insight that Assurance is an essential factor in salvation—not just an additional comfort which the saved man may hope to enjoy, but can very well get along without.

Assurance of salvation is essential, says Knox, because without assurance we must alternate miserably between hope and fear, never certain that we are acceptable to God.[1] But uncertainty and

---

[1] Preface to the treatise, *Works* V, pp. 21–30.

fear about our acceptability are distrust of God's redeeming mercy and love. And such distrust is the exact antithesis of the trust and self-commitment, of the faith in Himself and in His promises, that God calls for, and which are of the very essence of salvation.

We are saved by trusting God. But we are not trusting Him at all, so long as we doubt His assurance that we are acceptable, and are accepted by Him, for Christ's sake. To be told *that* in our inward hearts by God, is to have salvation offered to us. To believe it, when we are told it, is to be saved. Assurance therefore, assurance that God does accept us and has accepted us, is of the very essence of salvation.

Now, of course, if our acceptability to God depended on anything in ourselves—on the firmness of our faith, or the quality of our deeds—we never could have assurance. For our faith is frail, and our best deeds tainted with evil.

Assurance can only be reached (says Knox) when we realize that our acceptability with God rests on nothing in ourselves, but entirely on the election of God. And this election, since it proceeds from God's free and sovereign grace, and is exercised without respect to anything in us, does not vary with our changing moods, our successes or failures, our faith or our doubt, but abides constant and unchanging through them all.[1]

Election, therefore, is the true ground of assurance. Only conviction of election can produce such perfect trust. And perfect trust is essential; not only for the hour of conversion, but for the whole of the Christian life that follows after. For true service of God cannot spring from doubt and fear, but only from trust and love.[2]

The doctrine of election, then, produces Assurance—that joyful certainty that the love and mercy of God are ours—which was one of the new things that the Reformation brought to men. The mediaeval Church had awakened men to a profound and disquieting sense of sin. This sense of sin is indeed the leading factor in mediaeval religious life. But the mediaeval Church had signally failed to give men the assurance of salvation: it had taught

---

[1] *Op. cit.* pp. 26–27. [2] *Op. cit.* p. 30.

them to seek assurance through austerities and good works, and they had sought diligently and failed to find it. The Reformation, with its teaching that we are not saved by our works but only by God's gracious election of us to salvation, gave men the assurance they craved, and indeed required, for Christian living.

But it is an extraordinary thing that Knox did not clearly realize—none of the Reformers apparently realized—that by grounding assurance on election, rather than on merit, they were only pushing the problem of assurance back one stage, and pushing it into what appeared to be an even more terrifying form. For if salvation depends on merit, and I doubt of my salvation, I can at least do something about it: I can try harder to be good. But if salvation depends on God's election, and I doubt my election, I land in complete and hopeless paralysis. There is nothing I can do about that. If God has not elected me, what hope or help have I? Apparently none.

The first generation of Reformers, and Knox among them, had few doubts on this score. They had been led out of the "errors of Romanism" into the gracious light of the evangelical truth. They had known, in their own hearts, the reality of God's forgiving love. How could they doubt, in face of these facts, that they were elect to salvation?

It was only after the fire of this new experience was spent that gloomy doubts began to rise in some Calvinist circles. How could a man be sure that he was one of the elect? So long as a man could point to the fact that he had been led out of the "synagogue of Satan", and had braved persecution for the true faith, he could be persuaded that he was elect to salvation. But when Protestantism was established, and Tom, Dick and Harry were all Protestants, the question arose how Tom, Dick and Harry could all be sure that they were elect?

Knox was first seriously confronted with this problem in the person of his neurasthenic mother-in-law Mrs Bowes, and sorely he was perplexed both by her and by it. He treated her neuralgic conscience with extraordinary patience and gentleness; but I gravely doubt the wisdom of some of his pastoral counselling to her, and of the solutions he despairingly suggests for her recurrent doubts.[1]

He advocates the perilous method of self-inspection. Election should produce certain fruits, and if the fruits are there, we can be reasonably certain of our election. We must remember that even the elect may sin, and even sin grievously. Mrs Bowes is not, therefore, to despair of her election because of isolated lapses into sin. But if we find in ourselves a steady delight in some evil course, persistent wrong-doing, an ingrained aversion to god-liness, then we do well to doubt our election and to be seriously alarmed.[2]

But to what end should Mrs Bowes, or anyone else, be seri-ously alarmed, if everything depends on election, and election depends only on God's will, and on nothing in us? With sublime but perhaps saving inconsistency, Knox introduces at this point an exhortation to Mrs Bowes to "make her calling and election sure". It is not clear to me what he means by this. Clearly he does mean that greater efforts after righteousness are urgently called for in such a case. But is this because God's election of us is not final and decisive, but awaits confirmation in the light of our subsequent behaviour—so that it is never too late to mend?

This is to skate on very thin ice over the doctrine of merits, if not to crash through right up to the neck. To say this would indeed be a violent departure from his principles; though I should not put it past Knox to make it. The pastor in him was always mercifully strong enough to overcome the theologian in a really tight corner.

More probably, he means no more than that the spectacle of our progress in godly living will increase our own assurance of our election—assuming that we are elect. And in the case of Mrs Bowes he did assume that as beyond question; she could not have thought so highly of his sermons if she had not been elect. Yet, even to the elect, this is risky pastoral counselling: and it does

---

[1] A series of letters to her will be found in *Works* III, pp. 331-402.
[2] See also the Treatise on Predestination, *Works* V, p. 210.

nothing to meet the problem of those who have a basic and miserable doubt of their election.[1]

Surely the true answer to all such gloomy questionings is to get the victim to look outwards, not inwards. Assurance can never be internally grounded at all, but must rest altogether on the promise of God. The assurance is correlative to the promise, and cannot be introspected in abstraction from the promise. If God gives a promise, and I trust that promise—then I trust it, and that is the end of the matter. It is perversity thrice perverted to go on to ask whether my trust is a valid trust, whether my faith is a saving faith. It is a saving faith, if it believes a saving promise. It is a valid trust, if the promise itself is valid. Assurance of election can lie in nothing else than in the simple fact that we do believe in the mercy of God in Jesus Christ.

To seek to prop up this assurance by any other means than taking a closer and stronger grip on the Promise, is really to undermine and eventually to destroy it: to lead towards that miserable situation where men look into themselves for the evidences of election, and inevitably fail to find them. It would have been well if Knox had been clearer on this point than he was.

There is a related point on which Knox seems equally to waver, or perhaps rather to assert two sides of an antinomy with equal vehemence—the question of the Perseverance of the Saints: whether a man can fall from election, or whether election is final and irreversible, so that it must issue in full salvation.[2] To understand Knox on this point we must know something of what he means by free-will and obedience to God. He holds—and none has ever held it more strongly—that man's will is free. In a striking passage[3] in his Treatise on Predestination, he shows how Annas and Caiaphas, the Scribes and the Sanhedrin, Judas and Pilate, all acted freely in bringing about the crucifixion of Christ. Each man did precisely what he wanted to do, and purposed to do: yet, also, each man did precisely what God had predestinated

---

[1] Mrs Bowes's doubts on this point were pathological and incorrigible. She had an exasperating knack of discovering the weak spot in every argument that Knox designed for her comfort.   [2] *Works*, V, p. 210.   [3] *Works*, V, p. 142f.

him to do, in such a way that at the predetermined time, and in the predetermined way, Christ gave His life on the Cross for sinners. From all the ages, the Cross had been ordained, yet those who brought it about acted responsibly and freely in doing it.

The natural man, therefore, is free in all things but one. The one thing he cannot do is to obey God's will. He does God's will, unwittingly, because he is predestinated to do it. But obedience involves voluntary co-operation with the known will of God; and this the natural man cannot render, because he does not know the will of God, and would not do it if he did know it.

With conversion, obedience to the will of God becomes possible for the first time, for that will is now revealed to us in Christ, and is impressed in us by the Holy Spirit. But Knox is quite clear that the meaning of obedience is voluntary self-identification with the will of God. It would not be obedience if it was not voluntary. The whole difference between the elect and the non-elect at this point lies in the fact that the non-elect do God's will involuntarily, while the elect obey it voluntarily.[1] But does this mean that, after conversion, a man may fail in this voluntary self-identification with the will of God—may, by stubborn refusal to will God's will, reject the salvation that was his, and make his election of none effect? God can, and does, ensure that all men do His will, without infringing their freedom. But can even God guarantee a man's *voluntary* obedience and co-operation? Is it not clear that the redeemed man is free to withdraw this obedience, and so lapse from grace?

When Knox contemplates the Sovereign Majesty of God, he cannot believe this. What God has predestinated will come to pass. His election cannot fail. The saints will persevere unto full salvation, though they fall often, and sometimes (for a season) seem to fall away altogether.[2]

But when Knox contemplates the hearts of men, and his own heart, he is not so sure: and the pastor's voice rings out, calling men to watchfulness and care, lest in the end they be not found in the company of the redeemed. Once again, both sides of the anti-

[1] *Works*, V, pp. 144, 182.   [2] *Works*, V, p. 210; III, 364.

nomy are stated; and the anxious pastor corrects the confident theologian. Knox will have no man use the doctrine of the perseverance of the saints as a feather bed.

It remains to take a brief glance at the seamy side of the doctrine of Predestination: the matter of Reprobation. Knox grounds this partly on experience, partly on his understanding of God's nature, and wholly upon his understanding of the Bible.

Experience seems to show that while some men accept the Gospel, others steadily reject and despise it to their dying day, and delight in iniquity and mock at goodness. Since nothing in this world happens by chance, but all falls out according to the will of God, we must conclude that while God has elected some to salvation, He has reprobated others and predestinated them to damnation.[1]

Knox finds the reason for this double-edged predestination in the nature of God.[2] In Catholic theology, God had been regarded as substance. By the Scotists He was regarded as arbitrary will. The Reformers conceived of God rather as the embodiment of moral law, though the old conception of arbitrary will was not absent from their thoughts. The Calvinist system distinguished between the nature and the will of God; the stern necessity of justice belongs to His nature. By His nature, He is, and must be, just. But in His will God is absolutely free: and this divine freedom is expressed by showing mercy to those who would otherwise be the objects of God's stern justice.

But neither justice nor mercy could reveal themselves fully in a world that was devoid of evil.[3] Both the justice of God's nature, and the mercy of His will, require evil as the foil against which they can be displayed. God could not reveal Himself, in all His fullness, to a sinless humanity. All men must sin, in order that the elect may know His mercy, and all may know His justice. Hence God ordained the fall, creating man good, but giving man free-will, and ordaining that by the exercise of free-will man should fall.

[1] *Works*, V, p. 124 sq.   [2] *Works*, V, p. 406.   [3] *Works*, V, pp. 91–92.

Knox insists vehemently that Predestination must never be thought of as constraining man's free-will in the slightest degree —though by his own free-will man does exactly what God has predestinated him to do.[1] In this way Knox seeks to avoid the odium of making God responsible for sin. He fore-ordained it, but He did not compel man to it. Man was free, and therefore man was responsible. No doubt man could not have acted otherwise; but he did not desire to act otherwise. He sinned because he wanted to sin, and chose to sin. And (says Knox plaintively) how can people say that our doctrine of Predestination destroys man's free-will, when we keep insisting that man does just as he chooses, and exactly as he desires? Can you conceive of a will more free than that? This is not, of course, an attempted solution of the problem of evil, so much as an outright assertion of both sides of the antinomy: God is absolutely sovereign, and man is absolutely free. Man does just what he chooses, and, in so doing, does just what God chooses.

Confronted now by a fallen humanity, both God's justice and His mercy have free play to manifest themselves. Knox is fully prepared to cry "O felix culpa!"—O happy fault, that brought Christ into the world for our redemption! For had we not sinned and fallen, we should never have known all the greatness and wonder of God's mercy.[2]

But God's justice must be displayed as well as His mercy, for God is justice as well as mercy: and He cannot make Himself known without revealing His justice. Therefore, out of the mass of fallen humanity, God elects some to salvation, to manifest His mercy: others He leaves to their merited punishment, in order to manifest His justice. The reprobate are as necessary to God's self-manifestation as the elect. (This is the infra-lapsarian theory—that God's election operates on man as fallen, not on man as innocent. In a few passages Knox appears to incline to the supra-lapsarian doctrine; but on the whole, he is infra-lapsarian. Like Calvin, he had probably never thought the matter out.)

The principle by which God elects certain sinners to salvation,

---

[1] Works, V, pp. 41, 112f, etc.   [2] Works, V, p. 92.

and leaves others to their merited fate, is entirely opaque to us. It
is due to no quality in the sinners themselves, for all alike are
worthy of damnation. Yet Knox insists that the principle of
selection cannot be other than a just principle, since it proceeds
from a God whose very nature is justice. This is part of His secret
counsel which is too high for mortal mind to comprehend.[1] And,
as Knox very pertinently remarks, if we could understand why
God elects some and reprobates others, God would not be God.
God cannot be questioned on this point—not because His election
and reprobation are arbitrary and unjust; but because we could
not understand the answer even if we got it. All we can do at this
point is to lay our hand upon our mouths, and be dumb. Some
might be tempted to feel that Knox might with advantage have
laid his hand on his own mouth just a little sooner.

He may even have felt this himself: for it is a remarkable fact
that all this religious speculation is rigorously excluded from the
Scots Confession. Predestination is not discussed at all, and under
the heading of election[2] we are told simply that it was Christ who
was predestinated from all eternity to be our Saviour, and that we
are elected in Him. This passage in the *Scots Confession* rests so
directly on Knox's "anchor passage" in John 17—"Thine they
were, and Thou gavest them to me"—that I do not doubt that
here we have the simplicity of Knox's own faith: not a bowdleri-
zation of his views forced upon him by his more cautious
colleagues.

Knox can fly high in controversy, and speculate daringly. And
if men must speculate on such subjects (and I suppose that nothing
will ever stop them doing so) then I think that Knox's speculative
theology is worthy of a good deal of respect. But Percy is probably correct in his judgment that the Treatise on Predestination
was something of a *tour de force*, and that Knox's heart was not
really in it.[3]

Certainly, when he folds his speculative wings, it is to a simple
Christocentric faith that he returns—and to one that points

---

[1] *Works*, V, p. 114, etc.   [2] *Confession*, Cap. VIII.   [3] *John Knox*, p. 247.

towards that fine flowering of Federal theology which comes in Thomas Boston, a Scottish theologian whose work has too long been neglected.[1] Knox's Christocentric faith (and Boston's after him) is this: that the immediate object of God's election is Christ, not men. It is by Christ's calling of us, and in our union with Him, that we partake in this election of God. It is not ours directly, but only mediately, through Christ.

In this way, election does not by-pass and short-circuit the sacraments, as it does when stated speculatively. If we ourselves are the direct objects of God's election, then Baptism, and the Eucharist itself, must be emptied of much of their significance. For a man will then tend to rest himself on this eternal decree, rather than on any event that takes place in Time. But if it is Christ who is the object of election, and we are elect only in Him, then the sacraments in which we are united to Him grow and increase in significance.

I have already pointed out the stress that Knox lays on the Sacrament of Communion. The statement on election in the *Scots Confession* links up directly with this. It is in the Christo-centric, Johannine mysticism of the doctrine of election in the *Scots Confession* that Knox's true faith is displayed. One wishes that Knox, instead of writing that arid and speculative Treatise on Predestination,[2] had laboured instead at the rich mine of this, his own distinctive and personal comprehension of what election really means. Yet he points to where the riches lie; and others have gathered, and will gather, wealth from this mine.

[1] A new study of Boston and of Federal Theology, by Dr Donald Bruggink, is shortly to be published.

[2] To do Knox justice, it should be noted that the centrality of Christ in Election is by no means ignored in his Treatise on Predestination. Indeed, it is stated with peculiar force and beauty at one point—*Works*, V, pp. 50 to 54.

5

PROVIDENCE

5

Providence

IT must have become pretty evident, from what we saw of Knox's doctrine of Predestination in the previous lecture, that he would be bound to run into difficulties in his treatment of the Providence of God. That he should run into difficulties is not, of course, in the least surprising: any man who attempts to speak about Providence runs into difficulties, as every minister who has preached a sermon on that subject knows well. But Knox's very explicit views on Predestination add a peculiar edge and sharpness to these difficulties, and a peculiar danger to any hasty solutions of them.

You may remember that Knox excludes all chance from this universe. Nothing happens by accident; all falls out in the minutest detail as God has determined, and predetermined, it should. He will not even allow that God may permit certain things to happen which are not in full concord with His own will. There is no permissive or contingent will of God; God has one, unvarying will, and that will governs, absolutely, the whole course of events.

Knox escapes from what appears to be the inevitable consequence of this—the attribution of human wrong-doing to the will of God—by affirming just as vehemently the opposite side of the antinomy. That is to say, he attributes to man a freedom of will which we to-day, with our knowledge of the effects of heredity, of the subconscious, and of the influence of the ductless glands, scarcely find it possible to believe in.

Knox, then, affirms a paradox: that man's will is free; and that God ordains all events. And we may note in passing this further paradox: that the modern world, which finds it impossible to stomach Knox's predestinarianism, finds almost equal difficulty in believing in man's freedom and responsibility. Indeed it is a curious fact, and one worthy of some reflection, that human responsibility is most emphasized, and most strongly expressed in action also, under a predestinarian creed. We shall discuss the reason for this later in this lecture.

Meantime, we note that Knox believes absolutely in human freedom and responsibility: and that this relieves him of the necessity of ascribing to God responsibility for the evil and suffering that result from human sinfulness, and so eases for him one aspect of the problem of Providence. Thus, for example; if I foolishly disregard the rules of health, and thereby reap permanent invalidism, I may not blame God for my calamity. He predestinated this suffering for me, certainly; and predestinated it not in any general way—as a general law of hygiene—but specially and particularly for me. Yet I brought it on myself; and I, and I alone, am responsible for my sufferings. Knox holds, with Calvin, that God's predestination does not act coercively on men from outside, but works in and through men's choices and decisions; so that men both do as they freely choose, and also perform what God has ordained.[1] If I ruin my health, I bring myself by my own folly into the suffering that God has ordained for me. It is both my fault, and His will: my responsibility, and His predestination.

The same general principles hold good if I suffer, not through my own sins, but the sins of others. If a swindler ruins me, or armed violence brings suffering or death to myself or my family, these things are God's will and must be accepted as God's will. He fore-ordained them. But, at the same time, I must lay the blame where the blame belongs; and that is on the evil-doing of wicked men. They, not God, are responsible for what has happened to me.

We begin, now, to realize the subtlety of Knox's teaching on Providence; a subtlety that is seldom recognized or appreciated. It may not say the last word on this aspect of the doctrine of

---

[1] Treatise on Predestination, *passim*.

Providence (if there is a last word to be said); but it does one supremely important thing—it conserves a necessary place for the religious virtue of resignation, without withdrawing from man the right to rebel against evil, and, if necessary, to take action to terminate it.

I think that all who have been engaged in pastoral counselling will agree about the importance of resignation. The wounds in the soul of man are never truly healed, until he is brought to believe that somehow—even if he cannot understand it—his suffering is comprehended in the will and Providence of God. Not until that resignation to the will of God has been achieved, does the wound in the spirit heal cleanly and well. We need to see, or to believe, that there is a will of God in such sufferings, and to resign ourselves to it. That is an essential part of religion, and Knox's doctrine conserves it. Whatever happens to me is, without quibble or dubiety, God's will for me.

At the same time, I think most of us would feel—perhaps because we are the spiritual legatees of Knox and Calvin—that the matter cannot rightly terminate with pious resignation to the will of God. If the suffering has been caused by human wrong-doing, shall that wrong-doing be permitted to continue unchecked? As individual Christians, we are under orders to "avenge not ourselves" but rather to turn the other cheek to the smiter: and indeed all thoughts of personal revenge must be rigorously weeded out of our hearts.

But we are also citizens of our state; and to Knox as to all Calvinists, this is a truth of prime importance: and the state was ordained by God for, among other things, the restraint of wrong-doing. As citizens, we have therefore not merely a right but a religious duty to see that the swindler swindles no more, and that the armed "thug" is so dealt with that he can bring tragedy to no other homes.

If we feel in our very bones the force of this argument, it is largely because we are legatees of Knox and Calvin that we feel it. The man who rises from the sorrow of some personal injustice he has suffered, and campaigns not for personal vengeance but for legal and social reforms which will put a stop to such injustice, is in line with Knox, and probably has a heavy dose of Calvinism in his bones though he may not be aware of it. But of this we may say more in due course.

Meantime, we note the fact that Knox's doctrine of Providence conserves, on the one hand, the religious need for resignation; and on the other, the right and duty of protest. If we suffer through the wrong-doing of men, what we suffer is at once God's will, and man's responsibility.

Looked at in reverse, of course, this doctrine of Providence—with its discrimination between the will of God and the responsibility of man—enables Knox to declare that even the wrath and wickedness of man can serve the righteous purposes of God. The political assassin, his heart black with malice, may do (and indeed does do) the will of God when he strikes down a tyrant. And the observer, who sees a tyrant thus removed, may see in the event a notable and providential fulfilment of God's will, without being committed thereby to approval of the motives or actions of the assassin. In this way, perhaps, Knox could justify his openly expressed wish that some modern Jehu would arise to terminate the career of that bloody Jezebel Mary Tudor. But it must be admitted that Knox goes well beyond this in white-washing those who slew Cardinal Beaton, and murdered David Rizzio.

So far, then, we have examined Knox's doctrine of Providence on the relation between the will of God and the suffering that results from human sin. And we have seen that Knox holds that responsibility for all such suffering rests on man's shoulders alone, and so raises no acute problems for the doctrine of Providence.

The problems begin to come thick and fast, however, when we turn to a consideration of that vast mass of suffering that appears to have no human origin: the suffering that results from tempest and flood, from pestilence and failure of crops, and other such natural causes. All this comes by God's will, of course; but who is to take the immediate blame for it?

To be sure, there is always the devil, who has been a very

present help to many a theologian in trouble over this problem—for the devil supplies us with a will alien to God's will; and his power to bring about natural calamities, if it cannot be proved, cannot be disproved.

Knox, however, for a Scotsman, makes surprisingly little use of the devil in this connexion—so that I doubt Knox is not responsible for that easy familiarity with the devil which has been noted by many writers as a peculiarity of the Scots. The reason why Knox made little use of the concept of a cosmic evil will in handling the problem of natural evil lies, I think, in the fact that Knox thought of the devil as a force in the moral realm, rather than as a cosmic or elemental being of the Gnostic type. The devil was the leader and organizer of wicked men, almost the personification and embodiment of human evil: so much so that Knox seems to have felt that, in his own day and generation, Satan was practically incarnate in the Pope—"that pagan full of pride", sitting on the seven hills of Rome, forever scheming out plans for the persecution and slaying of the saints and the extinction of the Gospel, seducing kings and princes, and organizing them by incessant intrigues for that nefarious purpose. Knox's devil was not, therefore, elemental enough to explain natural evil. Knox could see Satan's hand in every form of moral wickedness; but in tempest, earthquake, famine or pestilence, Knox could see no other hand than the hand of God. God sends all these afflictions upon the children of men.

The modern theologian is somewhat shielded from the harshness of this view by his conception of the material universe as a semi-autonomous system, running machine-like under the control of natural laws laid down for it at the hour of its creation. He may—indeed if he is a Christian he *must*—believe that God is free to intervene providentially in His own universe when that intervention is necessary. But the natural laws are there: and natural calamities can be ascribed to their semi-independence which God cannot interfere with without upsetting the whole machinery of the universe. If an air-liner disintegrates in mid-air, it is not God but the law of gravity that kills the passengers: and God cannot be expected to wreck the universe by temporarily suspending that law in their favour.

But Knox has no conception of a semi-autonomous universe to ease for him this aspect of the problem of Providence. To his mind, the Sovereignty of God means that God rules in all things and all events. In all things that come to pass, the Divine Hand is directly and immediately at work. If tempest and flood bring destruction, if crops fail and famine stalks the land, this is God's doing. There is nothing and no one else who can be held responsible. And God is responsible not merely for the general catastrophe, but for the particular way in which it afflicts every man, woman and child involved in it.

On the other side of the account—when things go well, when the earth sweetly yields her increase, so that men prosper and their wealth increases—this also is the Lord's doing. And again, God is responsible not merely for the general well-being, but for that measure of prosperity which He allows to each particular individual. Both our prosperity and our adversity come directly from His hand: that is Knox's firm conviction.

But to the religious mind this poses the great, central problem of Providence: how shall we interpret such prosperity and adversity? Both come from the hand of God: why does He send them? What message do they carry? What do they mean? What lesson are they sent to teach us?

In the Old Testament, or at any rate in certain parts of the Old Testament, a very clear meaning is read into such events. Calamity is the expression of God's wrath against disobedience, and prosperity His reward for righteousness. God says by the mouth of Isaiah: "If ye be willing and obedient, ye shall eat the good of the land"[1]—and by Moses: "If ye do not these commandments ... I will make your heaven as iron, and your earth as brass ... your land shall not yield her increase, nor your trees their fruit."[2] So God had said in old time; and God does not change. Was it not

[1] Isaiah 1 : 19.
[2] Leviticus 26 : 14, 19f.; and cf. the appalling threats in Deuteronomy 28 : 15ff.

tempting to suppose that He who thus rewarded and chastised the Hebrews of old would so reward and chastise men in Scotland and England in the 16th century—and in later centuries too for that matter?

The temptation of such a belief to Knox must be obvious. It was manifest Scriptural teaching, with many a text to support it. To a preacher like Knox, who had to be constantly coaxing, threatening, and encouraging the fickle and the faint-hearted, it was just the precise message that was required.

Now it has been made a serious charge against Knox—and not only against Knox, but against Calvinism generally—that this is the characteristic Calvinist doctrine of Providence, and that this conception of divine reward and punishment by material prosperity and adversity became the religious basis and justification of later British and American capitalism.[1] Calvinism, everywhere it went, fostered a keen attention to business, and glorified business success as God's reward for righteousness—so it is asserted. Its doctrine of Providence inevitably has this prudential implication and appeal.

It is rather important, therefore, that we should investigate this charge against Knox, and against Calvinism, with some care, and see how far it may be justified.

It is true that, when we examine Knox's writings, we do find occasionally something that looks like this prudential view of Providence. There is an example of it in that sermon of his that so upset Darnley that he could not eat his dinner after it. It runs thus: "If we had heard the voice of the Lord our God, and given upright obedience to the same, God should have blessed us, He should have multiplied our peace, and should have rewarded our obedience before the eyes of the world ..."[2]

But when we look at it more carefully, we see that this is not really an example of the prudential view of Providence: for the

---

[1] See Tawney, *Religion and the Rise of Capitalism*, London, 1926; and Weber, *The Protestant Ethic and the Spirit of Capitalism*, New York, 1930.

[2] *Works*, VI, p. 242. Knox preserved this sermon as evidence for the legal proceedings which followed it. Most of his sermonic material he deliberately consigned to oblivion, believing that his message was for the day and the hour—not for posterity.

prosperity that would have rewarded righteousness is the spiritual prosperity of the Church—her peace, and the establishment of the Gospel. It does not even suggest that obedience would have brought bounteous harvests and business prosperity to the true believers. There is not the slightest trace of such a suggestion. And it is rather remarkable that in a sermon which lent itself readily to a prudential appeal, only such a spiritual appeal is found. The same is true of the prayers in Knox's Liturgy. The Providential blessings that may be expected to follow upon righteousness and obedience are blessings to the Church, or enlightenment for the nation, and are not of wealth or prosperity for individuals.

Knox, after all, was not so naïve as to be entirely unaware of the danger of connecting, too directly, a supposition of God's favour, or wrath, with man's prosperity or adversity. And if he had been tempted to postulate a simple causal connexion between them, Our Lord's words about those crushed by the fall of the tower of Siloam, about the man born blind, and about the perils and deceits of riches, were sufficient to make him pause. Knox was as well aware of these sayings as we are, and had pondered them at least as much as we have, and had learned their lesson. For in that same sermon to which I referred a moment ago, we find these words: "If quietness and prosperity make men not utterly to forget God, as David did for a season, yet it maketh them careless, insolent, and unmindful of what God requireth of them."[1]

Knox saw, with perfect clarity, that men assume far too readily, and quite wrongly, that prosperity is a divine blessing. To the worldly-minded it appears so; but the spiritually-minded should have eyes to see beyond that.

From Knox's summary of Balnaves' Treatise on Justification, I take the two following quite explicit and uncompromising statements:[2]

"Tribulations are profitable to the faithful" and "worldly tribulations are the sign and token of God's love." A prudential

---

[1] *Loc. cit.* p. 252.
[2] *Works*, III, p. 13. When Knox penned these words he was a slave in the French galley *Nôtre Dame*. As he says himself, they are not the words of "a speculative Theolog", but of a man in sore affliction.

interpretation of Providence could not be more explicitly denied than by that last sentence—tribulations, not prosperity, are the tokens of God's love.

Considering that we have before us these explicit disclaimers, and considering the difficulty of discovering in Knox's writings anything that might even suggest that material prosperity is a mark of God's favour, it is an extraordinary fact that we may nevertheless rise from a reading of Knox's works with a distinct impression that this is precisely what we have been told.

The reason is that although Knox does not say that obedience results in prosperity, he is constantly proclaiming that disobedience will result in calamity. And of course, if one reads, on page after page, of the calamities that must follow disobedience, one is bound to feel that if there had been no disobedience these calamities would not have followed. And from this one jumps to the conclusion that if there had been obedience instead of disobedience, the result would have been prosperity instead of adversity. There is no logical path to this conclusion; but there is a psychological path to it. There is an almost irresistible psychological pressure upon us to conclude that the man who says to us "If ye refuse and rebel, ye shall be devoured by the sword" means us also to understand that "If ye be willing and obedient, ye shall eat the good of the land."

I think that this may explain why so many people have the impression that Knox teaches, or at least encourages, a prudential view of Providence—that godliness leads to prosperity, and that affliction is a mark of God's disfavour. In fact Knox teaches the exact opposite of both propositions. He would rather say that all of us, the elect and the reprobate alike, are so sinful that we deserve to live in a state of permanent calamity. He would go further, and say that the elect, because they are sinful and frail, require regular chastisement to admonish them of their errors, and periodic trial to stiffen their faith. Indeed he goes even further in his Treatise on Predestination, where he states that the most striking examples of prosperity are found among the reprobate who are permitted to flourish and wax great in order that their final downfall may the more resoundingly proclaim God's justice and judgment.

Yet because of Knox's emphasis on the fact (or alleged fact) that sin will always lead to calamity, the psychological impression remains that Knox also taught the converse: that well-doing will lead to prosperity. And the suggestion has been made that Knox's teaching on Providence had something to do with the repulsive smugness of a much later generation of Scotsmen who regarded their own worldly prosperity as a sure mark of divine favour, and the misery of the poor as an inevitable mark and consequence of their unregenerate condition.[1] R. H. Tawney and Max Weber[2] have levelled the same accusation against Calvin and Calvinism in general, both in Britain and America, particularly with reference to the period of the Industrial Revolution.

Knox himself, as we have seen, must be exonerated from such opinions, whatever impression his writings may have made on others—and it is to be doubted whether they were making any impression at all in the Scotland of the Industrial Revolution.[3] As for Calvin, it is grotesque to suggest that his teaching had any such tendency. He teaches, directly, clearly and forcefully, the exact opposite. The following are only a few citations out of many that could be adduced, and they settle the question finally:—

"When prosperity is uninterrupted, it gradually corrupts the best of us."

"It is a diabolical misjudgment to suppose that when we see a man live at his ease, we may know thereby that he is in God's favour."

"Prosperity, like wine, inebriates men—nay even renders them demented."

"Prosperity is like mildew and rust to the godly soul: it is neces-

---

[1] Contrast Knox's solicitude for the poor—one of the most pleasing traits in his character. To his mind, the humble poor were especially under God's protection; and oppression of the poor would bring divine wrath on the community in which it was permitted.

[2] *Loc. cit.*

[3] See preface.

sary that we be subject, from first to last, to the chastisements of God."[1]

Surely no man, nurtured on such teaching, could be smugly complacent about his prosperous lot. Rather he would regard it with alarm, as a sign that God had ceased to strive with him for his salvation.

If it be asked what Calvin makes of the more material promises of the Old Testament, the answer is that he held, as Knox did not, a "developmental" idea of Biblical revelation, and therefore had a good deal less difficulty with them. All parts of Scripture were not on the same level. When God spoke to the ancient Israelites, He was speaking to those who were babes in spiritual things, and who had to be dealt with accordingly. The revelation was accommodated to their limited understanding. The promises, and the performance, were such as they could understand. For them it was true that those who kept God's commandments would receive material reward. But we are men in the faith, not babes; and our eyes are—or ought to be—more open to spiritual things. Our faith is to be tested by stronger stresses and longer waiting: and we are to find our blessing in the prosperity of the spirit, not in the prosperity of earthly riches.

The sanctimonious smugness of the rich certainly rests on nothing in the teaching of Calvin, and I am very far from being convinced that it was ever an exclusively Calvinist characteristic. No doubt it was found among Calvinists from the middle of the 17th century, right down through the period of the Industrial Revolution to the Victorian era. But it was found also in other denominations at the same time: among Lutherans on the Continent, and among sectaries in England who owed nothing to Calvin's teaching. And the high-priest and chief apostle of the doctrine was an Anglican—and a high-Church Anglican and stout Tory at that—the Rev. Dr Isaac Barrow[2] who held the

---

[1] Quotations from Calvin's Commentaries: On *Deuteronomy* 8 : 12, *Job* 21 : 7, *Hosea* 9 : 13, *Zechariah* 13 : 9 respectively.

[2] I am much indebted to Dr J. T. McNeill (*History and Character of Calvinism*, New York, 1954), not only for the reference to Dr Barrow, but for his illuminating discussion of the prudential element in Calvinism.

chair of mathematics at Cambridge before his friend and successor Isaac Newton. Barrow has a sermon with the significant title "Godliness is profitable" (I Timothy 4 : 8) and in the body of the sermon he proceeds to show that in very truth it is profitable, not only hereafter, but in terms of hard cash here and now. I cannot resist quoting two choice extracts from Barrow:—"Piety leads to preferments of all sorts, to honour, dignity, wealth and prosperity." And then, in discussing how generously God rewards almsgiving to the poor, he produces this gem—"Exercising bounty is the most advantageous method of improving and increasing an estate." What vials of indignation Calvin would have poured out upon such stuff if he had come across it! And what scorn Knox would have heaped upon it!

The case of the High Anglican Dr Barrow, and of others from other denominations, show that it is not necessary, and indeed cannot be right, to attribute this type of prudential piety to the influence of the Calvinist doctrine of Providence—which, after all, taught the exact opposite. It is rather an attitude which crept into all denominations as a result of the prudential climate of the times. Its only necessary ingredients are "a bit of money", some reading of the Old Testament, and a monumental ignorance of all that Calvin and Calvinism ever said about the Providence of God.

If it is true (which I doubt) that the attitude was more prevalent among the so-called Calvinist denominations than elsewhere, the reason might be that these denominations were more strongly represented among the social classes which were now rising to a position of affluence, and that they were therefore more strongly tempted than some others to seek religious sanction for their new-found prosperity. It is, of course, notorious that Calvinism fosters those qualities of sobriety and industry which—other things being equal—are likely to lead towards material prosperity. Presbyterianism may therefore have contained a higher percentage of persons liable to be tempted towards this aberration: but if they yielded to it they did so in spite of, and not because of, Calvinist doctrine.

Even in Scotland where, as I have said, Knox may have seemed to careless interpreters to give some colour to prudential views of Providence in his teaching, I doubt whether this really counted for much in comparison with the pressure of the mental climate of the times. Scottish Presbyterians were certainly no more prudential in their piety than was the High Anglican Dr Barrow of Cambridge who detested Calvin's teaching as much as Calvin would have detested his.

A word or two may be said in closing about the relationship between the doctrine of Providence, and history. In this matter the divergence between Lutheranism and Calvinism is considerable. Luther, as we saw in a previous lecture, began with the relationship between the soul and God; and this remained the centre of his consuming interest. Calvin began with the sovereignty of God over all creation and throughout all the ages. It would be an exaggeration, no doubt, to say that although Luther came out of the monastery, the monastery never came out of him: yet there is a truth in this. He remained a pastor and a father confessor, concerned with spiritual matters of the soul's relationship to God, content latterly to hand over all rule and authority to the state, provided he could shepherd his flock apart, in green and strictly spiritual pastures and beside still and entirely holy waters. After the Peasants' Revolt, his horror of any mingling of religion and politics grew almost pathological, and contributed largely to his hatred of the Swiss branch of the Reformation. Give him the souls of men: God had ordained the Protestant kings and princes to look after their bodies. Lutheranism thus tended to quietism, and stood aside from politics.

The Calvinist attitude was bound to work out far differently. Its fascination with the sovereignty of God attracted its gaze to limitless horizons. From the divine sovereignty, it passed to the divine decrees which govern the destinies not only of individuals but of nations, from time's beginning to time's end. Through all these ages, one divine plan and purpose unfolds. We can trace its development through all the pages of the Bible, and from the Bible we can learn something of the will and purpose of its

Divine Author. That mighty purpose sweeps down through the centuries to our own day. All men and all nations unwittingly serve it. But we, to whom the Holy Spirit, through Scripture, has revealed something of its meaning and purpose, can do something greater; for God is calling us to co-operate in the working out of His purposes.

This gives to the Calvinist a profound sense of the meaningfulness of the events of his times. God's Providence is seen not merely in the ordering of the life of the individual: much more it is to be seen in the ordering of great events, even political events, and of the individual's life in relation to these events. And the Calvinist knows (or thinks he knows) what these events mean, and whither, under God's Providence, they are tending. Knowing that, or believing he knows it, he feels himself called by God to co-operate to the uttermost with the divine purpose that is working out around him. And I need hardly point out to you that this sketch of the typical Calvinist is indistinguishable from the portrait of John Knox.

For such a man, of course, there can never be a rigid boundary line between religion and politics: for the same divine purpose runs and develops through both—and who should know better what that purpose is, than the student of the Bible and the preacher of the Word? It is not merely his right, it is his clear and manifest duty, to admonish rulers and politicians who are not in line with the divine will. Knox withstanding Mary, chiding Cecil, instructing Elizabeth, was not consciously presumptuous: he was —a Calvinist.

Furthermore, by this teaching Knox gave to his Scottish followers a standpoint from which they could criticize and evaluate the doings of their rulers. It would never be possible, after this, for a King on Scottish soil to substantiate a claim to rule by divine right, or to place his actions above review by the people. Any man with a Bible and eyes to read it, and the light of the Holy Spirit in his heart, could tell whether the King was doing the will of God or not: and if he felt any difficulty in reaching a decision, the pulpit was always there to give him guidance—

and seldom shirked what it felt to be its duty in that respect. It has never been possible, and it never will be possible, to prevent a Church which has a spark of Calvinism remaining in it, from scrutinizing the doings of governments, and passing judgments thereupon in the light of its understanding of God's will and His ordering of events.

But where men learn to think and judge on political and social matters, sooner or later they will consider it right that they should intervene in these matters and take a share in their management. Thus Calvinism, by an inner logic, tended towards participation by the people in political government, as from the start it had given them their part in ecclesiastical government.

6

THE FAITH OF THE HEART

6

The Faith of the Heart

NO one who studies Knox can fail to be struck by the mystery of the man himself; and the more one studies, the deeper grows the mystery. For here was a man who for twenty-five years lived in the full glare of the limelight—a controversial figure wherever he went, in England, Switzerland, Germany and France—a leader of great events in his own land of Scotland—the writer of one notable book and many lesser treatises: and yet how little we know of the man himself! We know only the face that he showed to the world, the outward appearance: the heart of the man we do not know. And it is not only we who are shut out from the secret; as we read references to him by his contemporaries, we feel that they too saw only the outside of him. He was to them a public figure—to be hated, or respected; but not, apparently, intimately known. Of George Wishart, by contrast, we have a revealing and touching little character study by one of his students, and we have a moving portrait by Knox himself; but no one has left a similar intimate portrait of Knox. To the outward impression he made we have abundant testimony: to the inner man, almost none.

The mystery extends even to the facts of his life before he became this "public figure". There are few historical personages about whose origins we know so little. We do not know with certainty where he was born. Until a few years ago, we were ten years wrong with the date of his birth. We thought his university was Glasgow—now we think it was St Andrews, though there is no trace of his name in the university registers there. And we do not know when the light of the evangel first dawned upon his mind. Part of the reason for this obscurity, no doubt, lies in the fact that he was of humble birth—of a class that keeps no family records. But Luther, too, was of humble birth, yet we know everything about his early days: the hymns he was taught at his mother's knee—the schools he went to—the impressions made on his mind by all sorts of childhood experiences. We know these things, because Luther has told them all: Knox has told us nothing. Not that Knox was ashamed of and attempted to conceal the obscurity of his birth: there was no point in concealing what all men knew and some cast in his teeth, and Knox took pride in recording that his father and grandfather had fought under Bothwell's banner. But of himself—his early experiences, his hopes, fears, aims, religious awakening—he tells us nothing.[1]

Luther is a striking contrast to Knox. Knox tells us nothing about himself; Luther tells the world everything. He is expansively autobiographical. He was so, partly by nature; but more so because his new found faith was hammered out on the anvil of his own experience, and he found it impossible to communicate it without communicating also the experiences through which he had reached it. His faith was so personal that he had to lead men by the road he came himself. If he wants to tell men of the wonder of the love of Christ, he must begin by telling of his own childhood terror of the frowning Christ with sword in hand in the stained glass window of Mansfeld Church. If he wants to describe the true nature of the Church, he must begin with his boyhood impressions gathered from the altar-piece at Magdeburg. If he wants to expound Justification by faith, he must tell how Martin Luther tried to justify himself by works as an Augustinian Eremite. To preach—to expound the faith—means, for Luther, to give a spiritual autobiography.

There is nothing in the least like this in Knox. His formal teaching is objective—entirely dissociated from himself. His *magnum opus* on Predestination, for example, could have been just as aptly signed "Bill Jones" as "John Knox"—so little does the writer

---

[1] Even his letters to Mrs Bowes, although they may dwell on his mood at the moment, are curiously scanty in autobiographical materials.

inject himself into what he writes. It would be the same, no matter who wrote it, so long as the writer was a Calvinist.

The same is true of the small amount of sermon material he has left us. The style, of course, is Knox's, and his alone. But it is objective truths he is handling, and his illustrations and appeals are to objective events that all men know. Of Knox's inner life, there is no mention.

In all this, he resembles Calvin more nearly than Luther. There is the same element of objectivity in Calvin; the same dissociation of doctrine from private and personal experience. But in Calvin this is not carried nearly so far. We know quite a lot about Calvin's early years. And he does describe for us, though not in great detail, the events of his conversion.

But in Knox this principle of anonymity and self-effacement is carried to a remarkable extreme. How can we account for it? Part of the reason, I imagine, is just that Knox is a Scotsman, and a very typical Scotsman at that. Percy suggests [1] (I will waste no time on Edwin Muir's opinions on the subject) that Knox had an inner mysticism—his true faith—about which he was wholly inarticulate, and which he could not communicate: and that alongside this he had a body of more "outward" doctrines or dogmas about which he could be very eloquent indeed. But this is a description not only of John Knox, but of almost any Scotsman who has any personal religion at all: get him on to some point of doctrine, and he will exhibit the notorious theological argumentativeness of his race: but try to probe into his personal faith, and he will either shut up tighter than any oyster, or speak with reluctance or even distress. Like the crab, the Scotsman wears all his bones outside: inside there is an unexpected emotionalism and sensitivity. John Knox was a very typical Scot, and his proverbial "crabbedness" was of this same type. He was not the type of man who would find it at all easy to reveal the secrets of his heart, on any subject, to the public gaze.

Yet there was another reason for Knox's reticence, and one which he shared with Calvin: namely, a keen sense of man's

[1] *John Knox*, p. 58ff.

littleness before God, and of the insignificance of the preacher, compared with the Word he preaches.

It was quite different with Luther. Luther started out from a very subjective and personal question: "How can I find for myself a merciful God?" And then he told the world how he had found that God. His theology was, in a sense, his own case-history expanded and made public.

Calvin, on the other hand—and Knox with him—start with the great and wholly objective spectacle of the glory of God Most High. To tell of Him—of His greatness, His mighty acts, His purpose of Redemption that sweeps down through all the ages, His sovereign commands, His purpose of love towards the elect in Christ—to tell all this was their message. And there simply was not room, in one small pulpit, for all this, and John Knox or John Calvin as well. Why should men, who have such mighty things to proclaim, waste time in recounting the insignificant spiritual pilgrimages of John Knox or John Calvin? Under the pressure of this great objective message, this Word of God, the preacher is effaced in his own consciousness, and becomes but the voice of one crying. ... The Scottish minister of our own day who said "When you go into the pulpit, leave yourself in the vestry" was of the same house and lineage as Knox. And this was Knox's own conception of his calling: this was the chief reason for his reticence and self-effacement—his conviction that his task was to be a voice crying to his own day and generation, and that alone.[1] The Word, the message was everything: the preacher was nothing. That, he tells us, is why he refused to preserve or publish his sermons: they were words for the hour, words from God to specific men in a given situation, not treatises by which John Knox was to be remembered by a future age. Let them accomplish that whereunto they were sent—and then let them perish.

When we speak of Knox's self-effacement, of course, we must guard against misunderstanding. It does not mean that Knox was in any sense lacking in assertiveness—very far from it. His message, he was profoundly convinced, was of vital importance.

[1] *Works*, VI, p. 229f.

Was it not God's own Word? And the voice that proclaimed it was an important voice, which men must hear. He was prepared to assert his message in the face of governors, and to let his voice ring in the ears of Queens. It mattered nothing whether they were pleased with what they heard or not: it was God's Word, and it was to be spoken to high and low equally, and with the same plainness. In that sense Knox was assertive—to many minds offensively so.

But it was the Word, the Divine Message as he understood it, that he asserted. Look where we will, we never find him asserting John Knox. No doubt we may feel that it was not the Word but "the Word as understood by John Knox" that was thus asserted. This is the failing of all preachers; and in a greater or less degree it is inevitable. The treasure comes in earthen vessels; and some clay—more or less—is always mixed with the gold. And no sane man will seek to deny that Knox mixed a fair amount of human clay with the heavenly treasure.

Yet this remains true—that Knox never consciously injected himself into his message: the reverse was true. Both by nature and by conviction he sought to obliterate what was private and personal.

This makes it an extremely difficult task to reach behind Knox's public pronouncements, and to make some exploration of his personal faith. We have little to go upon, for the materials are scanty, and the conclusions must be very tentative. Yet the figure of Knox challenges us to the attempt; for his influence over men can only be explained by a burning inward fervour—a spiritual glow—a faith of the heart—which is not fully expressed in the public acts and utterances which history records.

There is one clue to that inner life which I think it will be worth our while to follow up with some care. When he lay dying, he said to his wife: "Read where I cast my first anchor." His wife did not need to be told where to find it; it was a favourite passage —the passage which had given him his first grasp of the Gospel— St John, the seventeenth chapter. There, if anywhere, we may hope to find the key to Knox's inner life: for a man in the hour of death will go to that passage that holds the core of the matter for him.

And we find, when we go to that chapter, that verse by verse it illuminates Knox's life and teaching. We begin to see the perspective of his beliefs, the reasons for many things that otherwise are unclear, the true Knox behind the public figure.

The passage comes immediately after Christ's discourse to the disciples at the Table of the Last Supper. He has told them that He is about to leave them, and that they will all be scattered: that in the world they will have tribulation; "but be of good cheer; I have overcome the world."

Then, in the seventeenth chapter, there follows Our Lord's great prayer of self-consecration, just before He goes out to Gethsemane, and on to Golgotha. Archbishop Temple has called this seventeenth chapter "the most sacred passage, even in the four Gospels". A good place, indeed, for a man to cast his first anchor—and his last.

To test the hypothesis that the key to Knox's deepest convictions may be found in the seventeenth chapter of John, take a passage from one of his prayers and see how his devotional thought draws upon the passage from St John. Here is the Prayer:[1]

"Convert us O Lord, and we shall be converted. ... Though the great multitude remain rebellious, and although there remain in us perpetual imperfections, yet for the glory of Thine own name, and for the glory of Thine only beloved Son Jesus Christ, whose truth and evangel Thou of Thy mere mercy hast manifested among us: may it please Thee to take us under Thy protection and in Thy defence, that all the world may know that, as Thou hast begun this work of salvation among us, so of this same mercy Thou wilt continue it."

One may catch the echoes of Johannine phraseology, even

---

[1] From the *Book of Common Order; Works*, VI, p. 297. This prayer reflects Scottish conditions, and it replaces part of a prayer in the *Genevan Order* (*Works*, IV, p. 180) which reflected Genevan conditions. The prayer is full of Knox's favourite phrases, and is manifestly from his pen. Cf. his Thanksgiving Prayer—*History*, I, p. 332.

through the crabbedness of Knox's style. But there is more here than a correspondence of phrases, as we shall see when we set John 17 alongside the Prayer.

Take the opening phrase—"Though the great multitude of men remain rebellious." This is the background thought of all John 17 —the contrast between the world that knows not the Son, and those men who have known Him: "O righteous Father, the world hath not known Thee ... but these have known ..."

Then comes the petition—"although there remain in us perpetual imperfections ... yet take us under Thy protection and defence." This is simply a restatement of the 15th verse of John 17 —"that Thou shouldest keep them from the evil one." Our Lord's meaning is not that the disciples are sinless, and need only be kept from falling into sin. His meaning is that the Evil One still has a hold on them, and that it will require the constant, watchful care of God to rescue them ἐκ τοῦ πονηροῦ —"out of the clutches of the evil one". The Johannine passage might be rendered "Watch over them carefully, to shepherd them out of evil": and Knox says—"Though there remain in us perpetual imperfections, take us under Thy protection and defence." The language is different—the thought identical.

We then note Knox's phrase "For the glory of Thine own name, take us under Thy protection." This is simply a restatement, in the first person plural, of the 11th verse in St John: "Holy Father, keep through Thine own name those whom Thou hast given me."

Knox's next phrase: "Christ, whose verity and evangel Thou has manifested among us", is so typically Johannine that it could be drawn from almost any chapter in John; as for example "The Word was made flesh, and dwelt among us ... and we beheld his glory ... full of grace and truth." Verity and evangel in Knox mean truth and grace in John. But there is a specific enough parallel in John 17 itself—"I have manifested Thy name unto the men Thou gavest me ... I have given them Thy Word ... and they have received it."

Finally there is Knox's closing petition: "Take us into Thy

defence, that all the world may know that as Thou hast begun the work of salvation among us, Thou wilt continue it." This petition, of course, is a conflation of Philippians 1 : 6 with John 17, verses 21 and 23. Knox's thought is that the salvation of believers is a sign of God's power, and a testimony of His love, which even the unbelieving world will recognize. It closely follows Christ's prayer in John 17: "That they may be one in us, that the world may believe ..."—and again, "That they may be made perfect together, that the world may know that Thou hast sent Me, and hast loved them as Thou hast loved me."

Enough has been said to show how Knox's deepest devotional thoughts turn back towards the seventeenth chapter of St John's Gospel. It is not a literal dependence, as if he were merely copying out or remembering the passage. It is a dependence of thought. This passage has been so deeply meditated on, has so saturated Knox's mind, that its thoughts have become his thoughts. He thinks of God, and Christ, and salvation, and the life and vocation of the redeemed, in terms of Our Lord's great prayer of self-consecration.

Here, then, is our clue to Knox's inner convictions. Let us follow it up as far as we may.

When we begin to read through that seventeenth chapter, we are immediately struck—as Knox also must have been when he "cast his anchor" there—with the arresting words in the opening verse: "Father, the hour is come." What hour? The hour of Christ's self-giving on the Cross for the sins of men. And this is *the* hour—the hour for which all the ages have waited. All history before this has been leading up to this hour: all subsequent history is determined by it: and all Scripture witnesses to it. There is a process of redemption, proceeding through all time according to the divine plan; moving forward as God has ordained it, without haste, to one divine conclusion. And this is the central hour, the decisive event in the whole process. "Father, *the* hour is come"! No man who really casts anchor here can doubt thereafter that the mighty hands of God guide all history—or that Christ and His self-giving are the focal point which makes the whole process meaningful. He who grasps this has a key to both history and Scripture. He knows what the Bible is about—and, at least in outline, he knows what history is about too. The possibility unfolds of man's conscious co-operation with God in the fulfilment of His purpose.

Further, verse 1 and verse 4 make it clear what we do, when we thus obediently co-operate with the divine plan: we glorify God thereby—and this is man's chief end, for which he was created, and then redeemed. "I have glorified Thee on the earth," said Jesus, "I have finished the work which Thou gavest me to do. ... And as Thou hast sent me into the world, even so have I also sent them into the world." The work of the disciple is to continue the Master's obedient fulfilment of the divine plan, and thereby to glorify God. And the disciple knows, at least in outline, what the divine plan is—for "Henceforth I call you not servants; for the servant knoweth not what his Lord doeth; but I have called you friends; for all things that I have heard of my Father I have made known unto you."

Here lies the ground of Knox's conviction that he was busied about a great work. And here, perhaps, lies the reason for the accusation against him: that he seemed to imagine he was of the privy counsel of the Most High. The secularist, of course, can be expected to make nothing of any claims to a supernatural foresight of events—though secular historians do admit that Knox at times displayed remarkable political foresight. But if there is a God of righteousness, and if that God does exercise a providential government of the world, then certain consequences must sooner or later follow certain courses. Expediency and injustice may pay quick dividends; but they will end in bankruptcy. Wilful defiance of the purposes of God will wear out God's patience and be swept aside. And a man with prophetic insight, who has pondered deeply on God's ways as they are recorded in the Bible, might have not merely prophetic insight, but prophetic foresight of things to come. Knox believed he had such foresight on occasion, and I am by no means convinced that he was wrong.

We noted, in the lecture on Predestination, that Knox's basic conviction on this matter was clearly grounded on John 17. The only statement on Election and Predestination in the *Scots Confession* runs: "The Father elected us in Christ Jesus, his Son, before the foundation of the world."[1]

John 17, verse 24 runs: "Father, I will that they also, whom Thou hast given me, be with me where I am; that they may behold my glory, which Thou hast given me; for Thou lovedst me before the foundation of the world." Knox's Confession thus simply restates a verse from his "anchor passage".

His long Treatise on Predestination, with all its polemics, may have been a *tour de force*. Percy thinks that Knox found it almost as boring to write as we do to read. But though Knox may have had only an academic and polemical interest in a worked-out theory of predestination, he believed, from the bottom of his heart, in election. It was one of his sheet anchors—and election is the theme of this seventeenth chapter of St John.

The citations are too numerous to give: every other verse rings the same note—"Those Thou hast given me out of the world ... Thine they were and Thou gavest them to me ... that He should give eternal life to as many as Thou hast given Him." Even the dark side of reprobation is there. "I kept them, and not one of them is lost, but the son of perdition, that the Scripture might be fulfilled."

Here Knox took his stand; and here he based his faith. The world does not know God, and does not recognize His Son. But in this world there are men who belong to God, whom God chooses to give to His Son. No reason is assigned in Christ's Prayer for God's choice of these particular men. It must be out of "mere mercy", as Knox calls it, that God has chosen them. When they meet Christ, they know His voice and recognize that He is the Son of God. They do this, not in virtue of any particular qualification in themselves, but because of an inward illumination given them for this purpose by God's Spirit; "flesh and blood have not revealed it unto thee, but my Father which is in heaven."

[1] *Works*, II, p. 100.

Their election, their calling, their saving union with Christ, are all of sheer mercy, which must call forth their astonished and boundless gratitude.

If any man hears this call, recognizes the Son as Lord and Saviour, and comes into union with Christ, then he is one of God's elect. He did not choose: he was chosen. There is no presumption in his coming, no fear that he will be turned away. He is an invited guest, and all the power of God will keep him unto life eternal. There is nothing here to minister to pride or Pharisaism, but everything to minister to humble and thankful assurance: for all is of God's "mere mercy", and nothing rests on any questionable achievement of our own. This—which is at the heart of John 17—is the very citadel of Knox's hope.

So far, so good. The elect are drawn out of this blind and sinful world. But they are elect for a purpose. "Others"—as verse 20 makes clear—"are to believe through their word."

Yes, but who are these others? Undoubtedly others of the "elect", who have not yet heard the call. But what of the world itself—the world that lies in darkness, and rejects the Christ? Here we must surely believe that Knox tragically misunderstood his "anchor passage". Misled by the sharp distinction that is drawn here between the world and the followers of Christ, he assumed that that distinction was ultimate and absolute; that the world never can be saved, but only the elect be saved out of it. In his Treatise on Predestination he makes that plain: God loves not all men, but only the elect; and the Gospel of salvation is not for all men, but only the elect.[1] The world may hear, but it will not respond: only the elect will answer the call.

Thereby the sphere of God's love is tragically limited. On the elect He looks with love: but on the world with implacable wrath. And the elect ought to share that divine attitude. They also ought to hate the world that is at enmity against God. These are God's enemies: it is treason against Him if we treat them as our friends. Hatred of the wicked is thus not only permitted—it is enjoined. Not that this hatred should partake of personal spite: it

[1] *Works*, V, p. 61.

should be a high and holy anger against all the enemies of God that work iniquity, especially against those who oppose the Gospel (that is the Reformed Gospel), and seek to subvert the truth—the Reformed truth.

But one wonders whether human anger is ever high and holy enough to be safely indulged: and one wonders, in particular, whether Knox's was. There was surely, also, another text he had forgotten: "God so loved the World". Is not the message of John 17 greater than Knox dared to think—even this: that although the world is at enmity with God, rejects God, hates God, yet God has a purpose of love even for the world? To this end He gathers His elect; not just that they may gather other elect, but in order that they may so body forth Christ and His love, through their union with Him, that at last even the world may know and recognize the Christ? The elect are gathered in to form the Church: but the Church is created to gather in the world, out of its enmity. And even in its enmity, the world is not beyond God's love—therefore not beyond ours. To be sure, it stands in the "anchor passage": "that the world may know that Thou hast sent me." Knox thought this meant a reluctant recognition wrung from the impenitent and lost. It does not: it means the recognition of dawning faith. Even the world will know Christ savingly.

Here Knox failed: and here Calvinism failed right down to the time of our great-grandfathers. The Gospel was not for all—only for the elect. But in the providence of God, the consequences of that failure were mitigated by the Reformation principle that no man can draw the line between the elect and the reprobate: only God can do that. Therefore, although it was firmly believed that only the elect could answer the Gospel call, nevertheless the Gospel must be pressed on *all* men, lest haply they might be of the elect. The consequences of the theological error were not, therefore, so serious as they might have been expected to be.

Many other points can be noted where Knox's teaching manifestly rests on convictions learned from this greatest Johannine chapter. There is his understanding of what preaching is: "I have given them Thy Word." Preaching is not the delivery of a homily: it is the declaration of the Word given by God to Christ, and through Him to the disciples—a Word of power indeed!

There is his understanding of his commission—"As Thou, Father, hast sent me into the world, even so have I also sent them ..." He who preaches the Word is sent by Christ, and is the ambassador of a greater King than any earthly monarch. Shall he then alter the message delivered to him because it pleases not governors or princes?

But there is space to note only one further point, and this is the most important insight of all; the mystery of union with Christ. Here Knox's sheet-anchor is cast within the veil, and lays hold upon the eternal rock.

"This is life eternal, that they might *know* thee the only true God, and Jesus Christ, whom Thou hast sent"—so runs the third verse. This does not mean grasping a truth; it means communion with God through Jesus Christ. It means personal fellowship with Christ risen, living, and in the power of His resurrection.

If this be mysticism—to have tasted even a little of that communion with Christ which is life eternal, and to long with all one's heart and soul for more—then Percy is right: Knox was a mystic. But I do not care to call it mysticism, as if it were something altogether abnormal: I should call it the essence of Christianity, for this is what Christ holds out to all men if they will have it. And again, "mysticism" suggests the solitary visionary in his private rapture: and Knox has nothing of this in his make-up. He has learned something better from his seventeenth chapter of John, for the mystery of union that is spoken of there is always and only a corporate union: not solitary contemplation, but the communion of believers with Christ and in Christ. That is to say, it implies the Church, and requires the Church, and is fulfilled in the Church. "That they may be one"—prays Our Lord—"even as we are one. I in them, and Thou in me, that they may be made perfect in one. As Thou, Father art in me, and I in Thee, that they also may be one in us." The communion of the individual believer with his Lord is part, and a dependent part, of the communion of the Church in and with Christ. It is not something the individual contributes to the Church out of his private devotional life. No! Communion with Christ is found in and through the fellowship of the Church. Knox knows this: no man ever knew it better; and this knowledge makes him first, last, and all the time a Churchman—a passionate lover of the Church of Christ. Dear to him were the stones and the very dust of Zion.

But last of all comes the most sacred moment of the Prayer of Christ—and the heart of all Knox's faith. "For their sakes I consecrate myself," says Christ (that is, to the sacrifice on Calvary), "that they also may be consecrated in truth." This must mean that our fellowship with Christ must be in the fellowship of His sacrifice; must be the Communion of His body and blood. The Church's most sacred moment, and the most sacred moment of the individual believer, is when all, with united heart, take their places at the Lord's Table and in this sacrament become one Body with Christ the Head.

So Knox placed Word and Sacrament together, as he was taught by St John, as the twin pillars of the House of God—the Church. The Word has called us to Christ, and keeps calling us. And because we hear and keep hearing it, we gather time and again round His table, in wonder and awe, for the Communion that knits us all together with Him: the Father in the Son, and the Son in us, and we all one in Christ. Here is the centre of Knox's faith. Here was his supreme gift to the Scottish Church—that he made it not a Church of the Word only, but a Church of the Table as well. And so it has remained.

It is often said that the Reformation was a revival of Pauline Christianity; and so it was. But in the Scottish Church as Knox reformed it, there was added to the compelling power of the Pauline faith, the richness—the mystery—the wonder—of St John.

Index